COOK BOOK

FOOD PHARMACY

The Cookbook

A collection of anti-inflammatory recipes created in collaboration with the gut flora. Strengthens your immune system. To be stored within reach of children.

BOOST THE IMMUNE SYSTEM

Lina Nertby Aurell & Mia Clase

Photography Ulrika Ekblom

FOOD PHARMACY PRESS®

FOOD PHARMACY PRESS®
Riddargatan 20, 114 51 Stockholm, Sweden
www.FoodPharmacyCo.com

Original title Food Pharmacy Kokboken. En antiinflammatorisk receptsamling framtagen i samarbete med tarmfloran. Stärker ditt immunförsvar. Förvaras inom räckhåll för barn.

First published by Bonnier Fakta, Stockholm, Sweden.
English translation Harriet Cobbold Hielte
Photography Ulrika Ekblom
Layout Anna Lindelöw Mannheimer
Recipe development Therese Elgquist
Illustration (page 7) Anna Ileby. Other illustrations and components for the collages: Wellcome Images, wellcomeimages.org
Editor Linnéa von Zweigbergk
Prepress JK Morris Production
Print Livonia Print, 2020
ISBN 978-91-986064-1-6

CONTENTS

- But Mia, what sort of
a book is this anyway?

Long silence.

- This? Well it's a cookbook written
by two friends who began to feed the
good bacteria in their guts, became
obsessed by their research and
discovered that one can strengthen
the immune system with kale
and lasagne?

Lina smiles.

- Exactly.

FOODPHARMACYCO.COM
WELCOME!

HI! WE'RE LINA AND MIA. For a few years now we've been producing foodpharmacy.se, Sweden's largest (and only?) health blog with a focus on gut flora and anti-inflammatory food. We've always tried to be healthy but when three women close to us died far too early, in the space of one year, a "health angst" was born in us. And in the midst of our grief, we became more and more interested in what we ourselves could do to affect our health.

About the same time we got to know a professor called Stig Bengmark who has spent a large part of his life researching how the food we eat can strengthen our immune system. He taught us that chronic (also known as low-grade) inflammation is a common denominator in nearly all lifestyle related illnesses and something we should avoid if we want to stay healthy.

Professor Stig taught us that, due to our unhealthy lifestyles, many of us in the West unknowingly walk around with chronic inflammation. Luckily he also taught us that we have hundreds of billions of bacteria in our guts which, if we feed them right, are the foundations of a strong gut flora. This is one of our most effective weapons against inflammation, which isn't so strange since 70-80% of our immune system sits in the gut.

We've said it many times before but it bears repeating: Professor Stig opened a whole new world for us. Our meeting with him was the start of our pilgrimage towards a healthier life and we decided early on to share our journey. Something told us that there must be more people out there who, just like us, were interested in how we can positively affect our own health. Don't you think?

We had our answer and knew that the interest would be huge. Our little blog grew quickly from having two readers, dad Janne and mum Ann, to half a million in our first year. In conjunction with our first birthday we got our first book contract and in August 2016 we released our book, "Food Pharmacy: A Guide to Gut Bacteria, Anti-inflammatory foods, and Eating for Health". We could hardly believe it was true when our book rose quickly into the Top Ten lists and became one of Sweden's most sold books. And it didn't end there – within the space of a few months more than ten publishers from all over the world had bought the rights to our book. We looked at each other in surprise, realising Food Pharmacy, our little baby, had grown up to become a great role model.

Of course we were lucky with the timing. To be honest the main reason our book became such a success is the fact that so many people have had their eyes opened to how food affects their health, and want to learn more about how food can contribute to a healthier life. We believe the future is bright!

Now our first book has a sibling. The book you're holding in your hands is full of recipes that will not only lead to an immune system that has a lot in common with Fort Boyard, but will also force the biggest sceptic to reassess his old arguments for once and for all and open his eyes to the fact that healthy food can also be really delicious.

So what do you say, are you ready? Great, then let's go.

BOOST THE IMMUNE SYSTEM

THE GUT FLORA'S COMMANDMENTS

according to Food Pharmacy

01. Focus on what you can eat rather than what you're supposed to leave out.

02. Eat lots of raw vegetables in a variety of colours.

03. Go easy on the meat.

04. Indulge in green leaves.

05. Drink a green smoothie every day.

06. If you eat fish – choose wild.

07. Eat slowly and chew carefully.

08. Skip processed food.

09. Choose organic.

10. Increase the nutritional value through the use of germination and fermentation.

11. Lower the temperature a few degrees when you heat food.

12. Choose your fat carefully.

13. Pimp your food with herbs and spices.
14. Teach you and your children to indulge yourselves without sugar.
15. Become a nutrient hunter (and skip tummy fillers).
16. Give your body a chance to recover now and again through periodic fasting.
17. When you feel stressed, take a deep breath and try to focus on the positives in life.
18. Move!
19. Let food be your main source of nutrients but do supplement with vitamin D, omega 3 and synbiotics.
20. Enjoy! And don't be too hard on yourself. That's the most important thing of all.

Puh!

LUKE SKYWALKER'S ANTI-INFLAMMATORY KITCHEN

SCIENCE FOR YOU

ON OUR BLOG we often get the question: Who should we believe? This isn't a strange question at all. We live in a time when the media is constantly feeding us with different findings, added to which all the scientists seem to be saying different things. At least that's what we felt a few years ago. But then we scraped the surface a little. And we saw that it wasn't actually completely true.

You see there is one thing scientists are touchingly in agreement on – that the food we eat has an effect on how we feel. Sure the details are still debated: to which degree diet affects our health and which effect particular foods have on our health. For example one and the same foodstuff can protect against certain illnesses at the same time as encouraging others, similarly an item of food can affect our health positively up to a certain level and then suddenly become dangerous when taken above that level. But even if opinions differ on the nitty-gritty, research is actually in agreement on the big stuff. And if you're in the least bit unsure as to who you should listen to or are worried whether this book advocates yet another questionable diet, you can stop fretting now. There's one thing we can all be certain of – there is no research showing that a large and varied intake of plant based foods such as vegetables, antioxidant rich cereals, spices and herbs lead to anything other than better health. And that's the knowledge that lies at the heart of this book.

FOOD – A POWERFUL TOOL

Even though food is a fantastic tool for us to affect our own health it is of course important to understand that there are other factors deciding whether we get sick or remain healthy. Our health is decided by two factors: our lifestyle and our genes.

Food belongs of course to the first group, lifestyle, with other important pieces of the jigsaw being exercise, stress and sleep (to name a few). It can feel particularly hard to accept one has an unhealthy lifestyle because there can be so much needed to get to grips with to become healthier. Do you recognise yourself here? Just remember that small steps are better than no steps, the thing is to start somewhere. Additionally a healthy lifestyle in one area often leads to a better lifestyle in another. For example healthy food and regular exercise provide the right circumstances for a good night's sleep which in turn helps us to handle stress better.

When it comes to genes you have inherited a certain set that you can't change. But what you maybe didn't know is that it's been shown that our genes don't govern us to the extent previously thought. Research shows that we, with the help of our lifestyle, can, to a large degree, affect whether our genes are activated or not. This is called epigenetics. Remember that word.

To summarise we can establish that your lifestyle is made up of many factors, but that the food you actually eat is one of the most powerful tools that you yourself can use to influence whether your genes are activated or not. Nutritious food also supports the body's natural healing process when we've been unwell and can improve our prognosis. Basically you're not totally subject to your genes as we previously believed. The opposite in fact, if you're born with a slightly weaker genetic football team you still have considerable power over your own wellbeing.

Don't feel bad though if you, like us, haven't taken care of yourself in the best possible way. See instead all the possibilities – it's never too late to start. It's been shown that lifestyle changes can give great health benefits regardless of when you begin.

SCIENCE FOR YOU

Many of our lifestyle related illnesses could be partially or even completely eliminated with the help of our diet.

THE BATTLE OF THE GUT

Now, having established that lifestyle affects genes to a greater degree than we originally thought, we can take a closer look at what happens when an unhealthy lifestyle causes problems for our bodies. Let's say that you don't really take care of yourself, maybe you eat badly, are stressed, don't make time for exercise and you smoke – then, unfortunately, far too many of something called free radicals, are created. In small amounts free radicals are nothing to worry about, but if there become too many in the end the body can't defend itself against them. This leads to the immune system becoming exhausted and the body being affected by chronic inflammation, which is a risk factor and common denominator for life style related illnesses.

ROOKIE STYLE • FOR YOU •

Food Pharmacy ♥ Luke and his army of good bacteria. Luke and his army ♥ fibre (found in abundance in vegetables).

We think of it as an ongoing battle between the bacteria in your gut – a battle between your good Luke Skywalkers and your bad Darth Vaders. Your Lukes thrive on fibre. When you feed your Lukes lots of fibre they multiply fast and can start working. It's your good bacteria that extracts the nutrients from the food you eat and contributes to keeping inflammation in check. Through feeding your Luke Skywalkers you are basically helping your body build up a strong immune system.

Your Darth Vaders on the other hand grow strong on processed, nutrient poor food filled with e-numbers and added sugar. With an excess of Darth's bad bacteria your good bacteria disappears and your immune system is weakened. Since, unfortunately, it is this type of food that has dominated our food shops in recent decades it isn't exactly rocket science understanding that food is a big factor in why lifestyle related illnesses have increased so dramatically. But, even if you have ended up in bad eating habits all is definitely not lost. On the contrary, research has shown that it doesn't take long to alter your gut flora in a positive way. In certain studies one can actually see changes in the gut flora only a few days after starting to eat more healthily.

Do you agree with us that it it's a good idea to take command of your eating habits and begin to feed your Lukes instead of Darth's army? Or are you totally destroyed now that you've realised you don't fatten up your Lukes as much as you should?

In which case – take it easy and read on about Plato and his discovery, life will soon feel considerably lighter.

FOOD PHARMACY ❤ PLATO

In 300BC there lived a man called Plato. He was born in Athens, Greece, was a philosopher, mathematician and writer and strode up and down the streets with his index finger in the air. Perhaps you've heard how Platonism has shaped Western philosophy to a large degree? A good deal of Plato's philosophy goes under the name Platonic Idealism. Platonic Idealism is composed of two worlds: the Realm of Ideas (the pure form or ideal) and the Physical Realm (reality). According to Platonic Idealism nothing can exist in the physical world (reality) if there isn't a perfect ideal of it in the realm of ideas.

When we ran into Professor Stig and thereafter a long line of doctors and one or two science journalists, they supplied us with the research about how food affects our health. We can say they gave us the Realm of Ideas' view of food and "the ideal of the perfect plate". It was a good thought of course, but unfortunately our eating habits were pretty far removed from the the ideal and during our blog's first six months we went through all the feelings one goes through on realising one isn't perfect: shock, dejection, an inferiority complex and a heap of other unpleasant feelings. And in all honesty we didn't have a clue about how to handle it.

But then one day there came a knock on the door.

Mia turns to Lina.

- Can you open?

Lina reluctantly gets up from the sofa and goes to open the door. There stands Plato.

- Ave Lina. I'm very disappointus with you. You seem to have forgotten everything you learnt when you read philosophy at university.

- Ave Plato. Sorry, but I don't really understand what you mean. Would you mind refreshing my memory?

- Lina, Platonic idealism is about there being two worlds: the realm of ideas and the physical realm. You have to accept that you live in the physical realm. It's not possible to be perfectus in the physical realm. Accept this and see instead the ideal of the perfect plate as a goal. A goal you can aim for from your own abilities and personality. If you try to be perfectus you'll fail and then there is a great risk that you give up and continue living on cheese & onion crisps and pizza. Stop being so hard on yourself. You are but a human in the physical realm.

Lina exhales. Plato notes her relief and sighs heavily.

- I have noticed that people are so hard on themselves these days. There is no one who is the perfectus parent, delivers one hundred percent at work, has time to exercise every day, have a fabulous sex life and still have lots of time left over for their friends. Gain knowledge but don't be too hard on yourself. Content yourself with aiming for the realm of ideas. And when it comes to food think that you should do the best you can, from the conditions that exist that day. Take with you the best of the day. What did you do right? What can you continue to build on tomorrow? And forget everything else.

- Thank you for your words dear Plato. Now I know exactly what to do.

Lina comes back into the sitting room. Mia looks up from her laptop.

- God what a long time you took. Who was it?

- Oh it was just Plato.

- You look very calm and harmonious. It's making me feel quite irritated.

- No, don't be! I've just realised that we don't need to be perfect.

Mia, wide eyed, nods in agreement and holds up a glass of red.

After Plato's spontaneous visit we could, with the help of the Realm of Ideas and the Physical realm, approach our respective challenges in a way that felt inspiring and enjoyable rather than difficult. We tried as hard as we could, but didn't judge ourselves when things didn't exactly go to plan. And somewhere on our journey we took the opportunity, in close cooperation with our Luke Skywalkers, to create the gut flora's commandments according to Food Pharmacy (hope you saw them on pages 8-9).

A FEW LINES ON ENJOYMENT

Take a look at the commandments again. With Plato's words of wisdom ringing in our ears the last point in the gut flora's commandments became something of a motto for us on our journey. Life is short and one should have fun. Food is a big part of life. It should be enjoyed. If you enjoy it there's also a greater chance that the changes you make will be maintained. Are we agreed on that? Good, then let us be serious for a moment.

For at the same time as it's important to enjoy things we all benefit from challenging ourselves and pushing towards goals (now aware that they only exist in the realm of ideas). When we say you shouldn't set excessive demands for yourself it's not the same as setting no demands at all. Just make sure to do it at a pace that suits you and that you can maintain, and we promise you that the reward awaits you just around the corner. Had we only thought of pleasure and not strived towards something we would probably still have a Coca Cola in our hands and a fag hanging from our lips. Because the thing is, then and there, we were enjoying ourselves 100%.

Our problem has been that we have always believed there to be a conflict between the enjoyment of food and eating healthy food. What a misunderstanding – there isn't one at all! Tasty food can be healthy. Healthy food can be the most delicious you've eaten. It's just about trying things out. And slowly but surely we've learnt that even if it takes a little time, you can change. In the beginning we focused completely on what healthy things we could add rather than what we should take away. And suddenly we were discovering new tastes and ingredients that we loved. And maybe even enjoyed on a slightly deeper level this time as the new food made us feel good.

Another tip for you to take with you on your journey is that you gain a great deal by by enlisting an ally. Now maybe you eat a lot better than we used to but honestly it's doubtful this book would have been written if it wasn't for the fact that there were two of us. When Lina wanted to question everything and eat pavlova for breakfast, Mia could be there to bring her back on track. And vice versa. Thanks to our having a friend with us on the journey we could find some sort of balance on our rocky road to a healthier life (and speaking of rocky road you'll find a healthy variation on page 145).

PLATO'S PLATE MODEL

In the last few years, interest for so called anti-inflammatory food has grown and more people than ever have started to prepare food that calms inflammation and is full of fibre, antioxidants, vitamins and minerals, basically nutritious food without sugar and E numbers. And considering the connection between this and our health this isn't surprising.

To avoid inflammation and keep your Lukes in a good mood we've identified six keys. In our last book we delve into each key, but in this book we'll content ourselves with a shorter summary.

No 1
Teach yourself and your children that it's possible to treat yourself without sugar (but enjoy goodies every day)
We might as well be honest: sugar isn't good. The opposite in fact, sugar is really bad for us. Sugar is absorbed into the small intestine and your blood sugar is raised which in turn forces the pancreas to pump out insulin to lower the high levels. And when insulin levels are raised, the immune system goes into overdrive and over time wears out.

The good news is that this doesn't mean you have to eliminate sweet things for the rest of your life. It's just about choosing the right sweet things. Processed treats with white sugar, such as Kit Kats and Ben & Jerry ice cream, are out. But on the other hand you can replace them with lots of other healthier sweet treats.

Before we began eating gut friendly (we'll decide that's a phrase) we tried to keep our sweet tooth in check by only indulging at the weekends. But when we set out on our pilgrimage we discovered that it's possible to make goodies with natural sugars and that we could enjoy them nearly every day.

Dates, bananas and berries don't just make things taste sweet, they also contain antioxidants, vitamins, minerals and fibre which feeds the good bacteria in the gut.

No 2
Become a nutrient hunter (and say goodbye to tummy fillers)

Tummy fillers as we call them, are foods such as bread, rice and pasta. This sort of food is processed and as a result nutritionally poor, but it's not just this that's the problem. These foods act exactly like sugar does in the body, being absorbed into the small intestine which leads to the blood sugar being raised and forcing the pancreas to pump out insulin which wears out the immune system and leaves our army of good bacteria in the lurch.

Becoming a nutrient hunter is basically about replacing these foods with nutritious alternatives such as quinoa, sorghum and buckwheat. But most of all, allowing vegetables to take up even more room on the plate.

No 3
Indulge in vegetables (and get a party started in your gut flora)

Experts may be at odds over a fair amount of things but so far we've never met anyone who says that a large consumption of vegetables in all shapes and colours is anything but great for us. There is no doubt that vegetables are the best thing you can eat. Why? Well because they're full of plant fibre, antioxidants, vitamins and minerals – basically everything our Luke Skywalkers and an immune system could wish for.

The Swedish Food Agency advises us to eat 500 grams of vegetables a day, but many scientists think that we should eat significantly more than that. A new study which examined people whose intake of vegetables reached up to 800 grams a day, showed that the risks for a variety of illnesses decreased the greater the intake of vegetables. Many scientists suggest we should even be eating around 1 kilo of vegetables a day since they contain everything our good bacteria in the gut needs to create a rich gut flora, soothe inflammation and strengthen our immune system. Unfortunately only a minority

Vegetables are not just full of fibre, they contain antioxidants that counteract the free radicals.

of us reach the Swedish Food Agency's recommendations – the average woman eats 300 grams and the average man 250 grams.

No 4

Choose fat with care (and fight inflammation)

It wasn't that long ago we were scared of fat and swapped it for diet products but today we know that it's not the fat making us fat but mainly the sugar. Fat is vital – our organs need fat. But you must be aware that there is a difference between fat and fat. Unfortunately large parts of the world eat way too much animal fat and fats that are rich in omega-6 but poor in omega-3. It leads to sad Lukes, happy Darths, a weakened immune system and contributes to chronic inflammation and illnesses. You don't need to be scared of saturated fat (found in dairy and meat products) but if you are anxious about your gut flora you should go easy on it since it is hard to break down.

Instead eat lots of vegetable fats like avocado, nuts and seeds. Be sparing with oils and choose high quality ones such as cold pressed coconut, linseed and olive oils. Skip cheap oils rich in omega-6. Consider an omega-3 supplement, preferably krill oil. For those who eat fish, the fat found in fish such as wild mackerel, is one of the best fats we can eat.

No 5

Lower the temperature (preserve the nutrients and avoid the toxins created at high temperature)

Most of us know that a large part of the nutrients die when we heat food and that the higher the temperature the more of the nutrients are destroyed. What perhaps many don't know is that toxic substances are created when cooking at high temperatures. Heating leads to synthetic processes which create the possibility for new substances to form through two or more substances uniting. When foods are subjected to temperatures over 80-100c they acquire totally different properties than the originals and become, even if mildly, toxic.

So start to use the oven more and the frying pan a little less. Lower the temperature a few degrees and make a habit of always using coconut oil that can cope with high temperatures much better than other oils.

No 6
Give the body a chance to recover now and again (through periodic fasting)
Periodic fasting means that you shorten the amount of time during the day in which you eat and lengthen the time in the day in which you don't.

New research also shows that periodic fasting can be an effective tool to slow down the activation of undesirable genes – ie a practical example of how you yourself can make use of epigenetics and contribute to working against an undesired gene being activated. We were very happy to discover that it was enough to fast for a short period a couple of times a week. As long as you keep to a healthy diet otherwise the benefits are the same as if you fasted more frequently.

ROOKIE STYLE FOR YOU

Periodic fasting means that one supports the body's own daily detox.

SO WHAT DO WE EAT THEN?

We often refer to ourselves as nutrient hunters. Our focus when planning what to eat, other than that it should taste good of course, is to always consume as many nutrients as is possible. And so naturally the largest part of the meal consists of vegetables.

A common misconception, which we were the first to subscribe to just a few years ago, is that one can't make "real" food from vegetables and above all that they don't fill you up. We want to puncture that myth once and for all. We're full and we haven't had to ban any of our favourite dishes – by and large all of our favourite dishes can still be made despite the majority of the plate consisting of vegetables these days. For example we've learnt to make lasagne without pasta or meat (and actually without cheese too), meatballs without meat and cinnamon buns without sugar or wheat flour. And yes, all these recipes can be found further along in the book.

Something that many of the recipes in this book have in common is that they are quick and simple to make with few ingredients. Anything other would have been unthinkable given the lives we live. So that you don't have to buy a supply of different rarely used ingredients which are then left gathering dust at the back of the cupboard, we've made a conscious decision to use many of the same ingredients throughout the recipes in this book. As parents of small children we haven't the time in the kitchen we'd like. A good tip is to make extra dips to keep in the fridge and while already chopping vegetables to chop some extra for the next day.

The gut flora loves raw vegetables and this stamp makes it simple for you to find the recipes which are 100% raw.

Generally speaking one can say that the friendly bacteria in our gut loves all kinds of vegetables. They also love antioxidant rich alternatives such as quinoa, sorghum, buckwheat, potatoes and kelp noodles. They love beans, peas, lentils, nuts and seeds which not only enhance the taste but raise the nutritional content in any dish and they absolutely adore green leaves. Much of the nutrients sit in the peel, tops and stalks, which we used to throw away, and can be much more nutritious than the beet itself for example. Therefore, whenever possible, we avoid peeling vegetables and we like to use stalks and cores in smoothies and soups.

We always try to mix at least three colours when we eat because the different antioxidants (which are found in the colours) strengthen each other's properties.

When we understood that many spices are strongly anti-inflammatory we filled our kitchens with them. Dried spices went into the spice cupboard and fresh herbs ended up in pots, the fridge and the freezer. When we flavour our food with cinnamon, cumin, parsley, turmeric, oregano and coriander we raise the antioxidant content in any simple weekday meal.

We also noticed that we could prepare the same food but by swapping round the spices create a whole new dish. A kale soup with ginger and garlic doesn't taste like a kale soup with cumin and coriander. Another exciting discovery we made was that we no longer felt the need to use as much salt as before, our former ubiquitous spice.

Sometime we fry, we are but human, but now we're not talking about some burnt wok but rather frying at low temperatures. Sometimes we make soups and casseroles where certain things are heated (such as onion and lentils) and then mixed with raw vegetables in the blender. We call this half & half. A perfect tete-a-tete between the Physical realm and the Realm of Ideas.

We like to raise the nutritional content of the food through adding ingredients which are soaked, sprouting or fermented. In the Realm of Ideas we're forever sprouting things, but in the Physical realm we buy sprouts in the shops and add a tablespoon of fermented vegetables from the refrigerated section alongside our dinner. Something small is always better than nothing at all.

A small passage on how to ferment vegetables
Grate the vegetables with a cheese grater or food processor and place in a glass jar. Add a pinch of salt (without iodine). Work the vegetables so that the liquid runs. Put on the lid and let the jar stand in room temperature for a few days, up to a week if possible. Then store in the fridge and eat with everything.

!!!

If this is the first time you're looking in this book you might need to buy a few new ingredients. It's best to buy fresh vegetables as you need them, but dry pantry ingredients can be bought in larger quantities and kept at home so you're always ready! A pack of quinoa or lentils, a bag of nuts, dried spices and a bottle of vinegar not only last but keep for a good while. On the next page you'll find some of the staples we always have at home. Add some fresh, seasonal vegetables and then only the preparation remains.

Aside from the right ingredients you'll need a good blender or food processor to be able to make all the recipes in this book. Our blender is on the go all day and might, aside from our children, be what we love most.

HOW DO I USE THIS BOOK?

In this book we prescribe a little over 60 anti-inflammatory recipes, all produced in close collaboration with the gut flora. All the recipes are of course exquisite but we urge you to be creative. We may look respectable but in reality we're two true bohemians (not just in the kitchen) who more often than not cook according to how we feel that day, following our instincts rather than recipes. Often we don't have a clue what we're going to put in the blender or saucepan until we open the fridge and see what we have at home.

This is a cookbook for everyone – regardless of whether you are a family, or live on your own or communally, and regardless of whether you eat meat at every meal, now and then or are a strict vegan seven days a week. We ourselves are not vegans but all the recipes in this book are completely plant based with the exception of some egg here and there. For us the preparation of fish and meat was never a challenge, however we have found ourselves on more than one occasion staring at a turnip in total bewilderment. At the start of our pilgrimage we were totally committed to the idea of vegetables forming the base of every meal, the problem was just that we didn't know how to do this. Feel free to add fish, shellfish, meat or egg if you wish when preparing recipes from this book. The important thing is that vegetables form the foundation of our future meals, both from a health perspective but also out of concern for the environment.

LOOK OUT FOR THE STAMPS

In this book you'll come across a whole load of stamps. They're there to make things easier for you and point out which recipes are quick to make or contain large quantities of raw vegetables.

100% raw for you – The gut flora loves raw vegetables and this stamp makes it simple for you to find the recipes that are 100 percent raw.

Under 5 minutes – Oh yes, it's possible to prepare healthy food in under five minutes.

Half & half – This symbol shows which recipes are half heated, half raw.

Add prawns if you like - Add fish/prawns/tofu if you like – This symbol points out which dishes work particularly well with fish, prawns or tofu.

Works well in freezer – We often make double amounts and freeze the extra. This symbol shows which recipes are best suited.

FOOD PHARMACY STAPLES

Here's a list of our so called kitchen staples we always try to have at home. As far as it's possible we choose organic.

Vegetables and fruit
Everything! (including legumes such as beans and lentils)

For the pantry
Buckwheat
Buckwheat flour
Bean pasta
Chia seeds
Desiccated coconut
Kelp noodles
Nuts, all sorts
Oats
Pumpkin seeds
Quinoa
Sesame seeds
Sorghum grain
Sorghum flour
Sweet almonds
Whole linseeds

Herbs and spices
Basil
Black pepper
Cayenne Pepper
Chilli
Cardamom
Cinnamon (we use Ceylon cinnamon)
Cloves
Coriander
Cumin
Ginger
Oregano
Raw cacao
Salt and herb salt
Thyme
Turmeric (both fresh and ground)

For added flavour
Apple cider vinegar
Fish sauce
Honey
Sambal oelek
Tahini (we like the light best)
Tamari soya sauce
Vegetable stock

Other
Coconut milk/cream
Dark chocolate (at least 70 %)
Dates
Herbal tea (eg chamomile, yerba mate, peppermint)
Lightly or medium roasted coffee (extra important that it's organic)
Matcha powder
Nut butter
Oat milk (and other plant based alternatives)
Tinned chopped tomatoes
Tofu (extra important that it's organic)
Vanilla powder

Oils
Cold pressed coconut oil
Cold pressed olive oil

Supplements
D-vitamin
Omega-3
Probiotics and fibers

Prescription No.1

IN THE BLENDER

It's time for our first prescription. According to the Swedish Food Agency we should be eating half a kilo of vegetables a day but many of us don't even manage half of that. Using a blender is one of the simplest ways to consume colossal amounts of nutrients with the least possible effort. Every day we fill the jug with different sorts of vegetables, press start and hold our ears. Sometimes what emerges is a soup, sometimes a smoothie and sometimes a dip. And no, it's not a coincidence that this is the book's first prescription. If you're a rookie this is the best way to get going. Eat as you always do but add on a green smoothie every day. Or serve a dip or salsa alongside your normal supper. Voila you've raised the health giving properties of your meal by several degrees.

P.S. Don't forget that this chapter is also full of recipes for everyday meals!

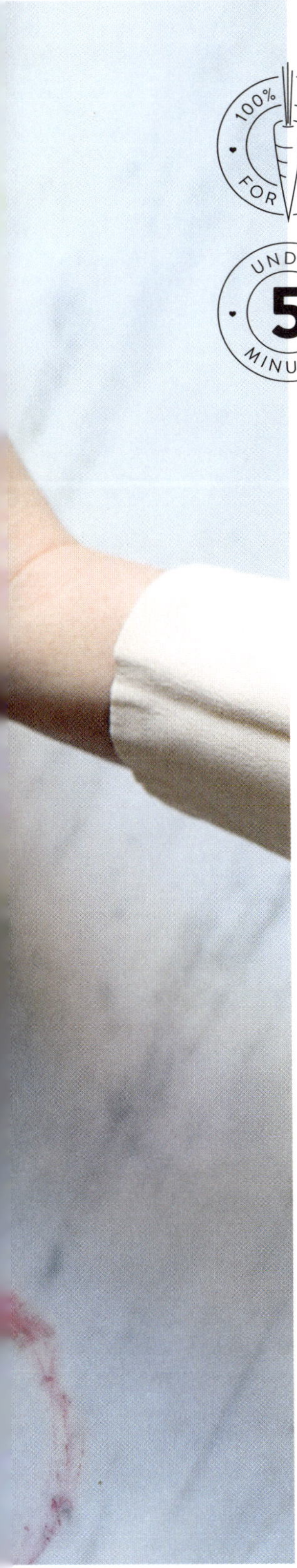

2 portions

A GLASS OF RED

Before we became inspired by a certain old philosopher we always had a glass of red wine on a Friday when we came home from work exhausted. Don't get us wrong, we still love wine, but we think that beetroot and celery together with creamy avocado, fresh mint and sweet dates isn't so bad either. And in contrast to that classic glass of red, after one of these you wake up full of energy. Cheers!

1 large beetroot (with the peel on)
1 avocado
1 stalk of celery
2 large handfuls of spinach leaves
10 fresh mint leaves
Juice from 1 lime
300 ml of water or your choice of plant based milk

Rinse the beetroot carefully. Peel and remove the stone from the avocado. Blend all the ingredients to a smooth smoothie.

QUICK TIP!

Blend a large handful of ice into the mixture just before serving for a cooling glass of rosé.

SCIENCE FOR YOU

Bought beetroots with leaves and stalks? Use them in the smoothie as well – much of the beetroot's nutrients sit right there.
And!
We prefer whole pieces of fruit or a smoothie to juice because in juice the important fibre is filtered away.

2 small glasses or 1 large

GREEN SECRETS

This is our best way of getting healthy stuff into our sceptical children without having to nag. Tastes sweet, contains greens, is pink. Everyone's happy, including our Lukes.

2 green bananas
1 avocado
250 g frozen raspberries
1 handful of baby spinach
200 ml water or your choice of plant based milk

Peel the bananas. Peel the avocado and remove the stone. Put all the ingredients into the blender.

Blend to a pink dream and serve with one pretty straw. Or ten, if the children get to decide.

ROOKIE STYLE FOR YOU

Other healthy ingredients that don't have a strong taste and can be sneaked into the smoothie: synbiotics, oats, pre-soaked nuts and bean sprouts.
And!
Imported frozen raspberries can contain norovirus. The Swedish Food Agency gives the advice to boil them for one minute.

100% RAW FOR YOU

UNDER 5 MINUTES

3
2
1
Tada!

100% RAW FOR YOU
UNDER 5 MINUTES

4 portions

SPEEDY CHILLI SOUP WITH TOMATO, LEMONGRASS AND COCONUT

2 spring onions (with stalks)
2 cm of peeled fresh ginger
2 garlic cloves
½ -1 red chilli
I stalk of lemongrass
800 g tomatoes (preferably plum)
1 tin of coconut milk (400ml)
1 tbsp Tamari soya sauce
Juice from 1 lime
300-400 ml water (amount according to preference and taste)
1 bunch of coriander (save a little for the garnish)

This is a fantastic soup, tailor made for lazy foodies. It works just as well for a dinner party as for a normal weekday lunch. If you have a good blender you don't even need to chop the vegetables – just cut into chunks, if you can be bothered, and press start. Use the time you've saved on chopping and prep to ponder over there being more stars in space than grains of sand on the whole earth.

Put everything, except the coriander, in the blender and blend till the soup looks creamy. Add some more water depending on how thick you want your soup.

Add most of the coriander (including the stalks) and pulse a couple of times. Pour into a saucepan and warm gently on a low heat.

Garnish with the rest of the fresh coriander. Enjoy!

QUICK TIP!

Tomatoes contain the antioxidant lycopene, the only antioxidant that improves when heated. Gently warming the soup releases the antioxidants in the tomatoes.

SCIENCE FOR YOU

Use the whole coriander in your cooking – the stalks taste just as good as the leaves.

100% RAW FOR YOU
UNDER 5 MINUTES
Pulse
KitchenAid

4–6 portions

RAINBOW GAZPACHO

1 cantaloupe melon (about 1kg)
1 fennel
4 spring onions (with stalks)
1 lemon
1 courgette
300 ml water
200 g ice (if you want an even more cooling gazpacho)
1 pot of lemon balm (save a little to garnish)
salt
freshly ground black pepper

In Spanish gazpacho means 'cold soup'. In Food Pharmacy's language it also means lots of fibre, antioxidants and vitamins. This little soup contains a whole rainbow of colours, remember to always mix at least three colours when you eat vegetables (since the qualities of the antioxidants of are strengthened that way).

On a different note melon is wonderfully thirst quenching in gazpacho.

Peel the melon and cut into chunks. Trim the fennel and spring onions and slice. Peel the lemon. Chop the courgette into big pieces.

Add water and blend everything except for the ice and the lemon balm. Add the lemon balm and ice and pulse a few times. Do save one little bit of melon which you can then dice to use as garnish alongside the extra lemon balm.

Season with salt and pepper to taste. Serve in deep bowls or glasses.

How to make

AN ANTI-INFLAMMATORY AVOCADO ROSE – STEP BY STEP

Today we're going to learn how to make an avocado rose! According to the internet it's easy as pie as long as you have a perfectly ripe avocado (which can be an achievement to find in itself).

1.

Peel. Start by spooning out one half of the avocado.

2.

Slice. Cut the avocado into thin slices with a sharp knife. Be careful so that the slices stay together rather than sliding apart.

3.

Shape. Carefully, carefully pull out the slices by squeezing the avocado slightly. Pull out the slices the whole way. The further you pull the easier it will be later to roll the avocado.

4.

Roll. Start rolling carefully, from the pointed end of the avocado.

5.

The finished rose! Yup, there it is. Easy as pie!

1 big bowl

GUNKAMOLE

Oh whatever, we'll make a good guacamole instead. We put in loads of coriander and it's usually gone in a trice.

½ red chilli
5 plum tomatoes
3 avocados
1 tbsp freshly squeezed lime juice
1 garlic clove
chopped coriander, according to taste
salt
freshly ground black pepper

Deseed the chilli. Finely chop the chilli and the tomatoes. Scoop out the flesh of the avocados and pulse in the blender along with the chopped chilli and tomatoes. Stir in the lime juice.

Peel and chop the garlic and stir into the mixture. Coarsely chop the coriander and mix that in too. Season with salt and pepper.

SCIENCE FOR YOU

A large part of the avocado's goodness comes from healthy, unsaturated fat which has been shown to decrease inflammation in the body.

4 portions

PSYCHO SOUP

Soup

500 g Jerusalem artichokes
½ leek
1.3 litre vegetable stock
400 g cauliflower
2 pears
2 tsp dried thyme
A splash of truffle oil (optional)
Salt
Freshly ground black pepper

Roasted Tuscan kale

80 g Tuscan kale
½ tbsp olive oil
1 g salt
Choice of fresh herbs such as parsley

You're maybe wondering what a psycho soup is. It's a soup that is good for both the gut and the brain. Research shows that good bacteria and fibre don't just get our gut flora in balance but also increase our mental wellbeing.

And speaking of fibre we can tell you that this soup contains Jerusalem artichokes and thus pectin, our good bacteria's fibre friend. In this recipe we cook the Jerusalem artichokes which makes them gentler on the stomach, but if you dare you can try adding them in raw towards the end.

Wash the Jerusalem artichokes and cut into small pieces. Rinse the leek carefully and slice into small chunks. Let the Jerusalem artichokes and the leek simmer in the stock until soft. Remove the saucepan from the heat and leave to cool a little.

Cut away the thickest part of the kale and shred the leaves. Massage these with oil and salt. Heat the oven to 100°C and roast the kale for around 40 minutes. Stir every now and again. Once done, set aside and save for the topping.

Cut the cauliflower and the pears into small chunks. Add this to the blender along with the stock, the rest of the vegetables and the thyme. Blend the soup till it is smooth and season with salt, pepper and a few drops of truffle oil. Warm the soup to a lukewarm temperature if that's how you prefer it.

Pour the soup into large bowls, drizzle over some more truffle oil if desired and top with the Tuscan kale, or, even simpler, some fresh herbs.

QUICK TIP!

If you don't have time to roast the Tuscan kale then just massage it with olive oil and salt for 30 seconds. The soup is also tasty just as it is!

HALF &
HALF

HALF & HALF
Where is the force when I need it!?

4 portions

THE ARMY'S KALE SOUP

1 yellow onion
2 garlic cloves
1 litre vegetable stock
200 g fresh kale
2 cm fresh ginger
½ lemon
1 tbsp cold pressed coconut oil
salt
freshly ground pepper

Have you got a second? Great, then we'll take the opportunity to remind you that a varied intake of vegetables is the key to a successful gut flora. In other words, you should dare to try new things not just eat the same things day in day out. The gut flora isn't like a car which only drives on one sort of petrol. Different bacteria like different sorts of fibre, and you can mix wildly without the motor cutting out.

Of course despite this you are allowed to favour certain vegetables. Kale for example. Kale is one of our absolute favourite vegetables, a weakness we share with Luke and his army.

Peel and chop the onion. Let it simmer in the stock until it softens. Take the stock off the heat and leave to cool a little.

Pour the stock and the rest of the ingredients into a blender and blend. It shouldn't be a completely smooth soup, it tastes best when there's some bite to it. Season with salt and pepper.

4 portions

BUTTERNUT SQUASH SOUP WITH A SHEDLOAD OF CORIANDER

1 kg butternut squash
1 yellow onion
2 garlic cloves
1 lime
1 tin of coconut milk (400 ml)
800 ml water
1 tsp ground cinnamon
1 pot of coriander (save a little for the garnish)
salt
freshly ground black pepper

Sorry but we can't control ourselves when it comes to coriander. Basically we can't get enough of it. What's more this soup contains one of the immune system's absolute favourite spices, cinnamon, which in turn contains lots of antioxidants.

And – how many times has one passed that squash in the food shop and not known what to do with it? Now you do.

Peel and cut the butternut squash into small pieces. Peel and chop the onion and the garlic.

Blend all the ingredients, apart from the coriander, in the blender till smooth.

Pour into a saucepan and heat the soup if you want but not too much, lukewarm is enough.

Finely chop most of the coriander and stir this into the soup. Season with salt and pepper. Pour into four bowls and garnish with the extra coriander. Not completely satisfied? Well add a bit more then.

SCIENCE FOR YOU

Cinnamon minimises the effect food has on your blood sugar. Good to think about when you're baking something sweet.

And!

The most common cinnamon, cassia cinnamon, is toxic to the liver in large amounts. Because we eat a lot of cinnamon every day we choose Ceylon cinnamon instead.

100% RAW FOR YOU
UNDER 5 MINUTES

How to make

THE ULTIMATE SUPPER SMOOTHIE

Time to throw out all those preconceptions about supper having to look a certain way. In this book one can look exactly how one wants to. (For a more formal recipe, turn to the next page.)

1.

Start by taking two large kale leaves.

2.

And an avocado and two stalks of celery.

3.

Oh go on, why not, throw on a lemon and some raw Jerusalem artichoke while you're at it. And a raw sweet potato. And a bit of ginger. And lots of green leaves.

4.

Close your eyes. Cross your fingers that the result tastes more of avocado than Jerusalem artichoke. Open your eyes and turn the page.

100% RAW FOR YOU

UNDER 5 MINUTES

About a litre

SUPPER SMOOTHIE

Voila, a pale green drink that tastes very green but tasty. Perfect for those days we can't be bothered to make dinner. If you're not used to green drinks and think the taste too harsh you can always add an apple or a kiwi. With the peel and pips of course.

1 small raw Jerusalem artichoke (with peel on)
1 small raw sweet potato (with peel)
1 small piece of ginger (with peel)
2 kale leaves (including the stalk)
1 avocado (including ¼ of the stone)
2 stalks of celery (including the leaves)
½ lemon (including peel and pips)
about 35 g green leaves of your choice
½ litre water

Rinse and scrub the root vegetables carefully.

Blend all the ingredients till completely smooth. Add a little extra water if you want your smoothie less thick.

SCIENCE FOR YOU

We love the taste of ginger. That it's been proved to be anti-inflammatory only increases that love.

And!

Don't forget the avocado stone holds lots of nutrients but only use max ¼ of it - otherwise the smoothie will taste bitter.

A selection of delicious

DIPS AND SALSAS

Question: What do you prefer to make with your vegetables?

1. A hardcore smoothie

2. A decorative pyramid that you can post on Instagram

3. A nutritious dip

Correct answer: There of course isn´t one. All the answers are correct, and yours is just as good as anyone else´s. But this time around, on the next page, we will just focus on the dip.

I Wanna Dance with Somebody
Whitney Houston

1 bowl (about 4 portions)

HERB HOUMOUS

1 carton of chickpeas (about 230 g)
1 garlic clove
2 tbsp light tahini
juice from ½ a lemon
3 tbsp cold pressed olive oil + extra to drizzle over
2 large handfuls of mixed fresh herbs
about ½ tsp of salt

Herb houmous goes well with most things. But we like it best just as it is with fresh vegetables.

Rinse the chickpeas. Peel and chop the garlic.

Blend the chickpeas, garlic, tahini and lemon juice to a smooth paste. Add 3 tablespoons of oil towards the end. Mix in the herbs and pulse a couple of times. Season with salt. Add a little water for a less thick houmous. Serve in a bowl and drizzle over a little extra olive oil.

SCIENCE FOR YOU

Did you know that chickpeas are an excellent source of calcium?

1 bowl (about 4 portions)

EDAMAME DIP

250 g green soya beans, thawed
½ garlic clove
1 pot of basil
2 tbsp of cold pressed olive oil
½ tsp salt
1 g freshly ground black pepper

Green soya beans, or edamame beans as they're called when still in their shell, are good to blend to a green dip. This might be our favourite recipe in the whole book.

Peel and chop the garlic. Blend the beans, garlic, basil and oil to a chunky dip. Season with salt and pepper.

QUICK TIP!

If you have sweet almonds at home you can add 50 g of soaked almonds to give a little crunch to the dip. Use almonds with their brown 'skins' if possible as that's where a lot of the vitamins are.

1 bowl (about 4 portions)

ANTI-INFLAMMATORY TURMERIC DIP

2 tbsp ground turmeric
4 tbsp cold pressed coconut oil
100 g pumpkin seeds
2 garlic cloves
1 tsp cumin seeds
1-2 tbsp tamari soya sauce
4 cherry tomatoes
the juice from 1 lemon
½ a pot of parsley
a little water
1-2 pitted dates (optional but yummy)
freshly ground black pepper

No one can really say no to a dip centred around the Zlatan of antioxidants. The Zlatan of antioxidants? Yes really. Turmeric contains an entire football team of antioxidants in which the most powerful is called Zlatan, sorry curcumin.

Blitz everything in the blender till it becomes creamy. Add a little water if the mix feels too thick.

Serve with raw vegetables or on the side of absolutely any meal.

300 g

OUR MAYONNAISE (WITHOUT EGG)

100 ml unsweetened soya drink
1 tbsp dijon mustard
1 tbsp white wine vinegar
200-250 ml mild cold pressed rapeseed oil
salt
freshly ground black pepper

Homemade mayonnaise isn't half as complicated as it sounds. It also keeps for a whole week in a clean glass jar in the fridge which is the best news we've heard in ages.

You can flavour it in 3,450 different ways (we've counted). A few ideas are to add 1 tablespoon of lemon juice, 1 tablespoon of tamari soya sauce or 1 teaspoon of sambal oelek.

Mix the soya milk, mustard and vinegar with a hand held blender.

Add the oil slowly whilst continuing to blend to a thick mayonnaise. If you want a stiffer mayonnaise you can add another 50 ml or so of oil whilst mixing.

Prescription No. 2

INSTEAD OF A SANDWICH

We've lived a large part of our lives on sandwiches. Had anyone told us a few years ago that we'd soon be able to manage without them we'd probably have bitten their heads off. The sandwich was our happy pill, our daily tummy filler, our crescendo in the Moonlight Sonata.

Today we hardly think about them. And however much we loved our bread we've realised that it over-shadowed all of the other snack options out there.

This chapter is for all those mealtimes where you used to eat a sandwich. Where once we'd have eaten a cheese toastie, we now choose one of the recipes from this chapter instead.

100% RAW FOR YOU

2 portions

YOGHURT WITH EXTRA GOOD BACTERIA – IN TWO WAYS

Speedy cashew yoghurt

200 g cashew nuts (soaked for at least 4 hours)
150 ml water
5 g synbiotics (1 sachet)

Slow coconut yoghurt

1 tin of coconut milk (400 ml)
5 g synbiotics (1 sachet)
1 tsp honey

One thing we never skip when cossetting our Lukes is sending in the big guns, synbiotics, once a day. Synbiotics are a supplement of good bacteria and fibre and a megaboost for your gut flora.

Speedy cashew yoghurt

Pour off the water the nuts soaked in. Blend the nuts and 150 ml of fresh water till completely smooth and creamy. Stir in the synbiotics. Done!

Slow coconut yoghurt

Put the coconut milk in the fridge for a couple of hours so that the coconut fat separates from the liquid. Save the liquid and put the setting lump into a clean glass jar. Thin with the saved coconut water till you feel satisfied. If, like us, you like the consistency of Turkish yoghurt then you should be fine with about 50 ml.

Stir the synbiotics into the coconut together with the honey. Put the jar, the lid slightly off, somewhere warm, above the fridge for example, and let it stand there for about 24 hours.

Stir and taste. If you want it even more sour it can stand for another 12-24 hours. It will keep in the fridge for five days.

ROOKIE STYLE FOR YOU

Was the yoghurt too sloppy? Stir and place in the fridge for a couple of hours.

And!

We use Professor Stig Bengmark's synbiotics, but there will of course be other brands in well stocked shops.

12 muffins

GOLD MUFFINS

Dry ingredients
200 g pecan nuts (soaked if possible)
250 g oats
150 g buckwheat flour
1 tsp baking powder
1 tsp bicarbonate
1 tbsp ground turmeric
1 tsp ground cardamom
½ tsp salt

Wet ingredients
2 small green bananas
1 small apple
1½ plant based milk of choice
75 ml cold pressed coconut oil
3 eggs

The only sweeteners in these muffins are banana and apple which means you can eat them every day. As usual we bake them at a low temperature so as to preserve the nutrients and avoid unnecessary toxins created by the heating process.

Best served with algebra or spelling tests. Beneficial to all homework!

Warm the oven to 100°C. Finely chop the pecan nuts. Mix in with the rest of the dry ingredients.

Peel the bananas and grate the apple. Blend the bananas, grated apple, plant milk and coconut oil to a smooth cream. Fold into the dry ingredients and stir. Whisk the eggs and mix into the batter.

Divide the batter into twelve muffin cases. Bake in the middle of the oven for about 1 hour. Use a stick to check if the muffins are ready.

QUICK TIP!

Top with lingon berries, press them down carefully so they stick. Or use raw cacao nibs, same technique.

ROOKIE STYLE FOR YOU

If you don't want to use eggs you can test with chia eggs instead. How do you make them? Google!

Just joking, here's the recipe for a chia egg: Mix 1 tbsp chia seeds with 3 tbsp water, stir and let stand for 10 minutes. Done!

WORKS WELL IN FREEZER
att läsa... tycker
jag. Ett stort pussel.
2000 bitar. Varför
jag vill ha 2000 b-
itar är för då kan
Om jag var stats-
minister, så vill jag

Learn to

CONJURE IN THE KITCHEN

Hello all you Paul Daniels out there – time for some magic!

1.

You will need: a carrot, banana, cinnamon, cardamom, ginger, plant based milk, walnuts and a blender. And a wand. (If you would like a more detailed recipe, please turn the page.)

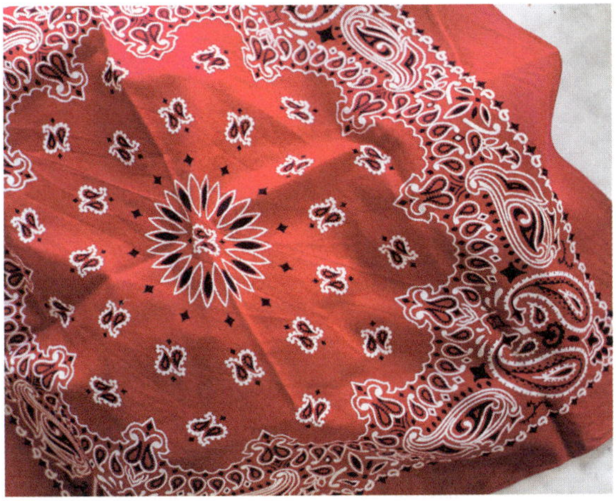

2.

Place a handkerchief over the ingredients.

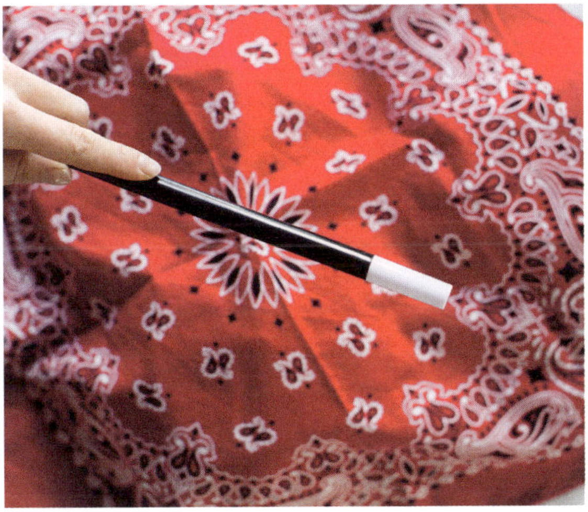

3.

Slowly move the wand clockwise whilst reading the following spell: Carrot carrot piranhabanana, kookaburra walnut tree.

4.

Look, the handkerchief moved! Absolutely crazy. Works every time.

2 glasses

CARROT CAKE SMOOTHIE

100% RAW FOR YOU

UNDER 5 MINUTES

This carrot cake smoothie will satisfy any sugar cravings and is made up of a wonderful armoury of anti-inflammatory spices. Yum!

1 carrot
1 green banana (frozen in slices if possible)
1 tsp ground cinnamon
½ tsp ground cardamom
¼ tsp ground ginger
6 walnuts (soaked if possible)
250 ml plant based milk of choice

Scrub the carrot and chop coarsely. Put everything into the blender and press start. Don't forget to read the spell on the previous page for the tastiest result.

SCIENCE FOR YOU

We always choose green bananas over yellow because green contain more of the wonder fibre pectin.

FOOD
PHARMACY
KIDS, RECEPT
Bästa pannkaksreceptet.
mjölk och

4 portions

BUCKWHEAT PANCAKES FROM THE PHYSICAL REALM

Pancakes
3 eggs
200 ml water
350 g buckwheat flour
500 ml plant based milk of choice
A pinch of salt
1 tbsp cold pressed coconut oil + extra to fry with

Apple puree
2 apples
4 dried soaked apricots
1 tsp ground cinnamon

Bean salsa
1 tin black beans (400 g)
½ red onion
1 avocado
250 g plum tomatoes
2 garlic cloves
½ pot of basil
salt
freshly ground black pepper

Sometimes we get nostalgic and go back through our blog and read old recipes. Funnily enough we've discovered that many of them are still favourites in the kitchen. Like our pancake recipe for example.

After a few compromises with Plato the idea of pancakes from the Physical realm was born. Serve them with the world's tastiest (and healthiest) apple puree, or skip sweet altogether and make a more substantial filling.

Pancakes

Whisk the eggs till fluffy.

Add the water, flour, milk and salt and whisk to an even batter. Melt the coconut fat in the frying pan and pour into the batter. Leave to cool for 10 minutes.

Pour a dollop of batter into the frying pan and cook the pancakes at a low temperature. Let them take their time.

Apple puree

Put the apples, including the peel and pips, into the blender along with the apricots and cinnamon and blend to a puree.

Bean salsa

Rinse the beans.

Peel the garlic and chop along with the tomatoes. Heat in a saucepan.

Peel and chop the red onion, take the stone from the avocado and cube the flesh. Mix the red onion, avocado and the warm tomatoes in with the beans. Season with salt and pepper.

Serve with the chopped basil.

2 small portions

GREEN CREAM

When we've tested giving our children completely green smoothies they've stuck their tongues out at us in an unbecoming manner. So we developed this green cream instead – a permanent ingredient in our weekly menu since. Banana, avocado and lemon form the base of the cream and then we sneak in one of the boosters below, their taste is neutral enough not to compete with the banana.

Works for breakfast, lunch or as a snack.

2 green bananas
1 avocado
juice from ½ lemon
1 handful of baby spinach, 100 g bean sprouts
or synbiotics

Blend.

QUICK TIP!

Add 1 tablespoon of raw cacao powder and ta da, you have chocolate cream.

2 portions

THREE KINDS OF EVERYDAY ICE CREAM

Chocolate ice cream – 2 portions
2 frozen green bananas
2 tbsp raw cacao powder
1 apple

Snickers ice cream – 2 portions
2 frozen green bananas
1 tbsp natural (unsalted and unroasted) peanut butter
1 tbsp raw cacao nibs

Strawberry ice cream - 2 large portions
1 packet (225 g) frozen strawberries
200 ml unsweetened plant based yoghurt of choice
1 tsp vanilla powder

In our families we eat ice cream nearly every day. Of course we're not talking about ordinary ice cream but ice cream that contains fibre, antioxidants and vitamins.

Lina's son likes the chocolate ice cream best. He eats it for breakfast. Before understanding that it was healthy ice cream he was eating in the mornings, Carl's teacher looked rather strangely at Lina. But she now knows what sort of ice cream we're talking about.

Chocolate ice cream

Peel and slice the bananas and freeze overnight.

Remove from the freezer and let thaw for a few minutes. Place in the blender together with the cacao and apple and blend to a creamy ice cream. Serve straightaway.

Snickers ice cream

Peel and slice the bananas and freeze overnight.

Remove from the freezer and leave to thaw for a few minutes. Blend in the mixer together with the peanut butter. Stir in the cacao nibs and serve straightaway.

Strawberry ice cream

Blend everything to a creamy ice cream. Serve straightaway.

100% RAW FOR YOU
UNDER 5 MINUTES

How to make

BREAKFAST IN BED

This recipe takes some time to be ready, and while we wait we take the opportunity to get our beauty sleep (we're clever like that).

1.

Invite a friend for a sleepover.

Mix oats, chia seeds, cinnamon, ginger, dates, desiccated coconut and plant milk in a bowl and put in the fridge.

(Turn the page for exact quantities.)

2.

Brush your teeth and don't forget to floss.

3.

Count sheep till you fall asleep.

4.

Sneak up and surprise your friend with breakfast in bed.

2 portions

FOOD PHARMACY'S GOLDEN PORRIDGE

This porridge is a crossover between overnight oats and the golden milk from our last book. So delicious, you have to try it.

200 g oats
2 tbsp chia seeds
2 dates (pitted)
1 tsp ground cinnamon
1 tsp ground turmeric
2 g ground cardamom
2 g ground ginger
50 g desiccated coconut
1 g salt
400 ml plant milk of choice

Cut the dates into small pieces. Mix all the ingredients together well and divide into two small bowls. Leave in the fridge overnight.

Remove from the fridge, stir and, if desired, add a little more plant milk for a thinner consistency. Sprinkle over a topping of your choice.

QUICK TIP!

Make extra of the spice mix so you skip making it afresh each time. Works brilliantly in porridge, smoothies and our golden muffins on page 58.

ROOKIE STYLE FOR YOU

Boost the porridge with blueberries, granola, apples or nuts.

100% RAW FOR YOU

UNDER 5 MINUTES

WORKS WELL IN FREEZER

15 balls

SPEEDY APPLE CAKE BALLS

Have you ever heard of anything as clever? Basically we take some of the classic ingredients of an apple cake, whizz them quickly in the blender and roll them into small balls.

One of the most common questions we get on the blog is what we give our children on school outings, and here you have the answer. Those times we haven't eaten them ourselves before they've made it into the rucksacks of course... But let's be happy that this time we managed to control oursel-ves and photograph them first.

1 apple
1 tbsp ground cinnamon
100 g sweet almonds (soaked if possible)
1 tsp vanilla powder
4-5 dates (pitted)
150 g oats
100 g desiccated coconut

In a food processor mix the apple, cinnamon, almonds, vanilla and dates to a crunchy batter. Stir in the oats and shape into somewhat even balls. Roll them in the coconut flakes.

SCIENCE FOR YOU

The good bacteria in the colon ferments beta glucan (the fibre in the oats) and forms a type of fatty acid that helps the body better handle the blood sugar.

Ordination no. 3

WEEKDAY MEALS

One of the most common prejudices about healthy food is that it's complicated. That one needs lots of time if it's going to be healthy and that it's tricky, near impossible, to manage on a weekday.

We suggest that it's more about habit. The trick is to exchange your five weekday recipes for five new ones that you demand the same things of: it has to be as quick to make, include as few ingredients and in principle you should be able to do it in your sleep. Instead of having meatballs and macaroni as your go to when you haven't the energy to think, you could try to make our pasta Napolitana. It's just as quick to make. It's just as simple. With one big difference: your Luke Skywalkers will be ever so much happier.

A pretty good reason to swap nutrient poor tummy fillers for sensible and nutritious weekday food if you ask us.

4 portions

PASTA NAPOLITANA

1 garlic clove
2 large tomatoes
6 sundried tomatoes
1 date (pitted)
50 ml cold pressed olive oil
1 tsp apple cider vinegar
2 tbsp pumpkin seeds
1 handful of fresh basil
salt
freshly ground black pepper

In Italy Pasta Napolitana is made with a lot of love and patience. In the world of Food Pharmacy we have unlimited amounts of love but no patience and above all only the tiniest amount of time. The only thing we really have in common with the Italian cooks is that we love tomato sauce.

Peel and chop the garlic.

Put in the food processor together with the tomatoes, date, oil and vinegar. Blend to a chunky sauce. Add the pumpkin seeds and basil and pulse a couple of times. Season with salt and pepper.

Heat to lukewarm if desired. Serve with the pasta or grain of your choice.

QUICK TIP!

In the Physical realm we serve the tomato sauce with whatever we want but in the Realm of Ideas we mix our pasta sauce with spiralized courgette.

SCIENCE FOR YOU

Heating gently before serving raises the antioxidants in the tomatoes.

And!

Think about not peeling the courgettes if you're making courgette pasta – the peel contains vitamin K (important for the skeleton) amongst other nutritious things.

1 minute
2 minutes
3 minutes
100% RAW FOR YOU
UNDER 5 MINUTES

WORKS WELL
IN FREEZER

4 portions

TACOBALLS

Tacoballs

1 carton of chickpeas (230 g)
4 carrots (with their tops if that's how you bought them)
2 tbsp light tahini
2 garlic cloves
1-2 tbsp taco spices (see recipe below)
2 tbsp cold pressed coconut oil
100 g oats
100 g white sesame seeds for rolling in

Taco spice (a big batch)

4 tbsp ground cumin
4 tsp paprika powder
4 tsp oregano
8 g ground cinnamon
2 tsp salt
1 tsp black pepper

When we ask our creative children what they want to eat for supper they always say two things: meatballs or tacos! Guess how surprised they are when they get both things at the same time!

We use both the carrot tops and their peel in these tacoballs so as to increase the nutritional value. For the same reason we bake them in the oven at a low temperature. We promise that they get the same lovely crispy exterior you'd get if you fried them in a normal frying pan.

Pour off the liquid from the chickpeas and rinse. Scrub the carrots carefully.

Blend the carrots, with their tops, to a crumb like consistency then add the other ingredients (except for the oats) and blend to a smooth batter. Mix in the oats and leave to swell for 15 minutes.

Heat the oven to 125°C. Shape around 20 balls from the batter and roll in the sesame seeds.

Place on a baking tray lined with baking paper and bake in the middle of the oven for about an hour. Turn the balls after half the time. Serve with your choice of pasta or grain and our tomato sauce from the previous page.

Taco spice

Mix together all the ingredients and store in a jar with an airtight lid.

ROOKIE STYLE FOR YOU

We stick stubbornly to light tahini in this book. Dark tahini works just as well, we just happen to think the light is a lot nicer.

And!

Use sprouting chickpeas for even more goodness!

4 portions

PARENTS' CARROT PASTA WITH A KICK

Cashew sauce with a kick

100 g cashew nuts (soaked for at least 2 hours)
3 dates (pitted)
1 tsp vegetable stock powder
1 tsp curry powder
1 g of ground cayenne pepper
100 ml water
salt
freshly ground black pepper

"Pasta"

6 large carrots
1 broccoli
250 g cocktail tomatoes
70 g baby spinach

Tamari roasted pumpkin seeds

4 tbsp pumpkin seeds
2 tbsp tamari soya sauce

Ok, we're now going to take all the prejudices you may have about healthy carrot pasta and crumple them into a little mental paper ball that you set alight. This pasta is actually one of the most delicious things on earth.

We thank our friend Ulrika who introduced us to this interesting dish. It's almost too yummy for its own good. Stop reading and start cooking.

Heat the oven to 80°C. Put the pumpkin seeds on a baking tray. Sprinkle the tamari soya sauce over the seeds and roast for 30 minutes. Stir around every now and then.

Drain the cashew nuts and blend in a food processor along with the dates, stock powder, curry powder, cayenne pepper and water. Season with salt and pepper.

Scrub and wash the carrots and peel into long pieces of 'spaghetti' and place in a bowl.

Boil water in a saucepan. Break the broccoli into small florets and steam in a colander with a lid for 3 minutes.

Cut the tomatoes in half. Mix the carrots, broccoli, tomatoes and spinach with the cashew nut sauce. Divide between four plates and scatter the pumpkin seeds on top.

ROOKIE STYLE FOR YOU

This sauce with a sting also goes wonderfully with courgette noodles, kelp noodles and bean pasta. Just choose your favourite!

100% RAW FOR YOU
ADD TOFU IF YOU LIKE

How to prepare

LEFTOVERS

Tralala, what a beautiful day! The sun is shining and everything suddenly feels so easy. We'll go home and prepare that Bimbimbu from page 122 even though it's the middle of the week.

1.

Once home we suddenly change our minds.

2.
Maybe we won't make that Bimbimbu after all.

3.
Lord, can we even be bothered to make dinner at all?

4.
Perhaps we should just eat the leftovers from yesterday?

2 adults and 2 children

FOOD PHARMACY'S CHINESE NOODLES

We often make double of this because it tastes even better after a day in the fridge (and because sometimes there's no better feeling in the world than not having to cook during the week).

Works for both big and small. What, you think the children are going to protest? Don't be too sure about that. Promise to try in any case!

1 tbsp cold pressed coconut oil
1/3 white cabbage head
1/3 cauliflower head
1 whole small broccoli
1-2 carrots
2 garlic cloves
1 red onion
1 yellow pepper
50 ml tamari soya sauce
2 tbsp sesame oil
100 g cashew nuts
1 packet kelp noodles (about 300 g)

Take a large saucepan and add a splash of coconut oil.

Chop all the vegetables and put them in the saucepan. Place over a low heat and stir now and then. Add the tamari sauce and sesame oil, little by little, to taste. Leave on the hob for about 15 minutes.

Serve with cashew nuts and noodles.

ROOKIE STYLE FOR YOU

If you're in a particular hurry, prepare the dish with frozen vegetables (with the same flavourings).

And!

This dish works perfectly as half and half. The pepper, cauliflower and broccoli can be thrown in just before serving.

4 portions

LASAGNE FROM THE REALM OF IDEAS

Lasagne

100 g sundried tomatoes in oil, drained
1 pack firm natural tofu (c. 270g)
100 g walnuts
1 tbsp tamari soya sauce
1 pot of fresh basil
2 aubergines
1 yellow onion
1 garlic clove
1 tbsp cold pressed coconut oil
2 tins of chopped tomatoes (c. 400 g)
2 tsp dried thyme
2 tsp dried oregano
1 tsp dried basil
2 tsp apple cider vinegar
herb salt
freshly ground black pepper

Pumpkin parmesan

100 g pumpkin seeds
1 tbsp nutritional yeast
½ garlic clove, peeled
1 tbsp cold pressed olive oil
2 g of salt

To serve

Green salad (a mix of baby spinach, chard, rocket and lamb's lettuce for example)

Five hours drive south of Stockholm lies a small coastal town called Kalmar. In this town there's a little house which holds a very special place in our hearts. It's where large parts of both our books were written. Thank you Karin and Kristofer for lending us your home, promise not to panic if you find a few red stains in the kitchen. It's not blood. It's lasagne.

Roughly chop the tomatoes. Pour the liquid off the tofu and squeeze out the water.

In a food processor blend the tomatoes and walnuts to crumbs, add the tofu and pulse to a crunchy "mince". Add the tamari soya sauce and most of the fresh basil (save a little for the garnish) and pulse a few more times.

Slice the aubergines very thinly lengthways with a cheese slicer or mandolin. Boil water in a saucepan. Steam the aubergine slices in a colander under a lid for a couple of minutes. Remove and dry the slices with kitchen paper.

Heat the oven to 100°C. Place a spoonful of mince at the bottom of each aubergine slice and then roll up. Place all the rolls in an ovenproof dish.

Peel and finely chop the onion and garlic. Gently warm the chopped onion and garlic in a frying pan with a little oil. Add the tinned tomatoes, the dried herbs and the vinegar. Season with the herb salt and the black pepper. Pour the tomato sauce over the aubergine rolls. Bake in the middle of the oven for about 30 minutes until the aubergine rolls are soft and the tomato sauce has reached a lukewarm temperature.

Blend all the ingredients for the pumpkin parmesan. Top the lasagne with fresh basil and half of the pumpkin parmesan. Serve with a simple green salad and the rest of the pumpkin parmesan on the side.

QUICK TIP!

If we're in the Physical realm we buy ordinary parmesan instead.

HALF & HALF
WORKS WELL IN FREEZER
ADD SHRIMP IF YOU LIKE
ADD FISH IF YOU LIKE

4 portions

THE FAMILY'S MANGO CASSEROLE

1 yellow onion
3 garlic cloves
2 cm fresh ginger without peel
1½ tbsp ground turmeric
1 tbsp cold pressed coconut oil
1 tin of chopped tomatoes
50 g tomato puree
200 g cashew nuts (preferably soaked)
1 tin of coconut milk (about 400ml)
salt
freshly ground black pepper
1 mango (or 250 g frozen mango, defrosted)
1 packet firm natural tofu (c. 270 g)
400 g plum tomatoes
70 g baby spinach
½ pot coriander for serving (optional)

One windy afternoon in November the doorbell rings. Lina's daughter Ninni runs and opens the door. It's Plato.

– Good dayus Ninni, here I am with the world's most delicious recipe for a mango casserolus.

Ninni calls out in disappointment:

– Mummy, some weird guy in a sheet wants to talk to you.

Peel and chop the onion and garlic. Heat the onion, garlic, ginger and turmeric in the coconut oil in a saucepan on a low heat.

Pour everything in the ingredients list up to the mango into the blender and blend until it becomes gritty. It shouldn't be a perfectly smooth, velvety sauce, in fact bits will only add character and make it better.

Pour the sauce back into the saucepan, heat till it becomes lukewarm. Cut the mango and tofu into pieces and add to the saucepan. Halve the tomatoes and add to the sauce along with the spinach.

Garnish with the coriander and serve with boiled sorghum, quinoa or buckwheat.

ROOKIE STYLE FOR YOU

This casserole can be made a day in advance and will keep in the fridge for about four days.

4 portions

COCONUT BREADED FAKE FINGERS

Fake fingers

2 packs firm natural tofu (about 270g each)
tamari soya sauce
1 egg
100g desiccated coconut
Cold pressed coconut oil for frying

Salad for grown ups (and cool kids)

1 grapefruit
1 avocado
2 spring onions (including stalks)
1 fennel
70g lamb's lettuce
½ a pot of mint
juice from ½ a lime
2 tbsp cold pressed olive oil
2 g salt
freshly ground black pepper

One annoying thing that comes up when starting to change food habits is that one quickly realises that the obvious weekday meals don't really cut the mustard. As a result we've become experts at creating new versions of our old weekday heroes. So now, when the children demand fish fingers we serve them fake fingers.

Squeeze the water from the tofu. Cut into slices, coat in the soya sauce and the beaten egg and then the grated coconut. Put to one side.

Warm a little of the oil in a frying pan and add the breaded tofu. Fry the fake fingers to a light gold colour on a low heat.

Peel the grapefruit and cut into chunks. Peel, pit and slice the avocado. Chop the spring onions and thinly slice the fennel using a mandolin or sharp knife. Place the grapefruit and vegetables onto a dish with the lamb's lettuce. Mix together a dressing of chopped mint, squeezed lime, olive oil, salt and pepper and pour over the salad.

Serve the fake fingers and salad with your choice of mash or puree (for example sweet potato and garlic puree or potato and Jerusalem artichoke mash, page 109).

ROOKIE STYLE FOR YOU

Fennel and grapefruit work well with all sorts of fish and shellfish!

SCIENCE FOR YOU

The white membrane which encases each section of the grapefruit holds lots of nutrients so don't remove it.

ADD FISH
IF YOU LIKE
1
2
3
4

WORKS WELL IN FREEZER

4 hearty burgers

BEETROOT BURGERS WITH EXTRA EVERYTHING

Beetroot burgers
1 tbsp chia seeds
+ 3 tbsp hot water
4 medium sized beetroots
(c. 300g)
½ red onion
2 garlic cloves
200g oats
½ pot of basil
50g capers
juice from ½ lemon
salt
pinch of freshly ground
black pepper

Herb mayo
100 ml mayonnaise
(see page 53)
1 handful of herbs, or 2 small
handfuls of different herbs
(eg basil and parsley)

To serve
salad leaves
quick pickled red onion,
see recipe on page 107
cashew coleslaw,
see recipe on page 107

1998 was an exciting year – the EU decided to introduce the Euro as a currency and Monica Lewinsky accused Bill Clinton of sexual assault. But most importantly of all we went to New York with our besties Runken and Angelica.

Like the urbane 20 year olds we were we ordered new exotic dishes at every restaurant we visited. But not Angelica. Breakfast, lunch and dinner – burgers. The winner? Angelica of course, who was served one fantastic burger after the other.

This fab veggie version is for you, Angelica. Just as greasy as you like it.

Heat the over to 100°C.

Mix the chia seeds with the hot water and let swell for 5 minutes.

Scrub and finely grate the beetroots. Peel and finely chop the onion, peel and grate the garlic. Chop the basil and capers. Combine all the burger ingredients well. Add a little water if necessary. Leave the mixture to stand and swell for 30 minutes.

Shape the mixture into four big burgers (or more smaller). Place on a baking tray lined with baking paper and bake in the oven for 25 minutes. Leave to cool a little before serving.

Mix together the mayonnaise and stir in the herbs.

Serve the burger between the crispy salad leaves together with the herb mayonnaise and our quick pickled red onion and cashew coleslaw.

Important information

HOW TO MASSAGE KALE

The secret behind a really soft and tasty kale salad is to massage it first. Time to take your kale to the spa!

1.
Begin by offering the kale a shower and a towel.

2.

Tear the kale into small pieces and settle comfortably in a bowl with olive oil and sea salt.

3.

Pamper your kale with a two minute massage.

4.

When you feel the tension slipping away and the leaves start to soften the kale is ready.

4 portions

FOOD PHARMACY'S UNIVERSAL SALAD

Now that you've massaged the kale you can do two things: 1) Spread them on a baking tray covered in baking paper and put them in the oven at max 100°C for about 30 minutes till you get crisps, or 2) make our lovely universal salad. By universal we mean you can eat it as it is, add yummy things willy-nilly or exchange any of the listed ingredients for another you prefer.

150 g massaged kale
200 g quinoa
1 punnet of cocktail tomatoes (200 g)
2 garlic cloves
cold pressed coconut oil for frying
1 red onion
1-2 avocados
1 tin of chickpeas (400 g)
juice from ½ lemon
salt
freshly ground black pepper

Place the kale in a salad bowl.

Cook the quinoa according to the instructions on the packet. Cut the cocktail tomatoes into quarters and peel and chop the garlic.

Add a splash of coconut oil to a saucepan and warm the garlic and tomatoes for a few seconds.

Peel and chop the red onion. Slice the avocado. Pour the tomatoes and garlic over the kale together with the red onion, avocado, chickpeas and quinoa. Squeeze the lemon over the salad. Season with salt and black pepper.

4 portions

PAD THAI SALAD WITH SCRAMBLED EGG

Vegetables
2 medium courgettes
2 carrots
½ small red cabbage
1 small cauliflower head
2 spring onions (with stalks)
200g mung bean sprouts

Peanut sauce
100g peanut butter
2 tbsp freshly squeezed lime juice
1 tbsp tamari soya sauce
1 cm fresh ginger without peel, finely grated
4 tbsp water

Scrambled tofu
1 pack firm natural tofu (c 270g)
1 tbsp cold pressed coconut oil
1 tbsp tamari soya sauce

To serve
Natural (unsalted, unroasted peanuts
Fresh coriander
Lime

Everyone loves our pad thai. Well, everyone but Darth and his army of course. Top this salad with spicy scrambled tofu to provoke them even more.

Oh and we've noticed that a version of this sauce (a little less lime and ginger) is usually a hit with children. One tip is to massage the sauce into vegetables the children usually like. Or simply put it out as a dip when serving vegetables. Maybe this sauce can get them to eat vegetables they would otherwise never have tried?

Start by peeling the courgette, carrots and red cabbage with a cheese slicer or potato peeler into long spaghetti like strips (or use a spiralizer if you have one).

Cut the cauliflower into smaller florets and slice with a mandolin or sharp knife. Slice the spring onions. Stir all the vegetables in a bowl together with the sprouts. Put to one side.

Mix together the ingredients for the peanut sauce. Add half the sauce to the vegetables. If possible let stand for 1 hour before serving so that the flavours really sink in.

Mash the tofu with a fork to a "scrambled eggs" like consistency. Warm the tofu on a low heat in a little coconut oil till lukewarm. Remove from the hob and pour the tamari sauce over the top.

Divide the vegetables between four bowls. Place the tofu on top, drizzle over a little of the peanut sauce and top with chopped peanuts and coriander. Serve the rest of the sauce, and extra lime, on the side.

ROOKIE STYLE FOR YOU

If you have time, let the vegetables marinate in the peanut sauce overnight so they can really suck up all the flavour.

4 portions

FAB PATTIES

100 g uncooked whole sorghum grains (300 g cooked)
2 courgettes
1 garlic clove
½ pot chives
1 egg
4 tbsp buckwheat flour
2 g salt
1 g freshly ground pepper

In Gothenburg, Sweden, where we come from, the school dining room isn't called a canteen. It's called the bamba. As the cherry on the cake our school held a competition for the students to name our bamba. The student council received hundreds of suggestions and a month later a winner was chosen. "La Bamba" was born.

These fab patties have absolutely nothing in common with the meat patties served in La Bamba except for the shape and the word patty. Apart from that: two totally different patties.

Boil the sorghum grains according to the instructions on the packet or use precooked. Let cool.

Grate the courgettes coarsely and put in a colander. Sprinkle on a little salt and leave to drain for about 20 minutes. Squeeze well to extract all the water from the courgettes.

Peel and finely grate the garlic and finely chop the chives. Mix the courgettes with the garlic, chives, egg, sorghum and buckwheat flour. Season with salt and pepper.

Warm the over to 100°C. Portion out the batter in small dollops (about 2 tablespoons each) on to a baking tray covered with baking paper. Flatten lightly with a spoon and shape into patties. Bake in the middle of the oven for about 60 minutes.

Serve the patties with a big green salad.

ROOKIE STYLE FOR YOU

In the Physical realm it has happened that we've smuggled a little feta cheese into the batter. Or why not serve with roe and crème fraiche if it's a party (and Plato isn't invited)?

100% RAW FOR YOU
MEGA
BOOSTER
KIMSJI
FOOD PHARMACY
COLESLAW

A gang of delicious and

SPEEDY BOOSTERS FOR THE GUT FLORA

Question: What do quick pickled red onion, kimchi and cashew coleslaw have in common?

1. They're tasty

X. They're good for the gut flora

2. You can't overdose on them

Correct answer: All the answers are correct. Please turn the page for more detailed instructions.

1 large jar

FOOD PHARMACY'S SPEEDY KIMCHI

1 small Chinese cabbage (about 1 kg)
3 carrots
100 ml white wine vinegar
1 tbsp finely grated ginger without peel
1 tbsp sambal oelek paste
1 tbsp fresh garlic, grated
½ tbsp salt

Kimchi is a common side dish in Korea and is addictively tasty and super healthy due to it being fermented. "Ordinary" kimchi takes at least a couple of days to make, but this variety needs only a day and minimal effort is required.

Cut away the root from the cabbage and shred the leaves finely. Put in a colander, add salt and massage well. Let stand for 15 minutes and then press out the excess liquid.

Scrub the carrots and grate coarsely. Massage all the ingredients together in a bowl (use plastic gloves if you want), till the vegetables begin to release their liquid.

Pack the mixture down hard into a clean glass jar and pour over the vinegar. Press down firmly an extra time so that the liquid rises up and covers everything. Fill a little plastic bag with water and place on top as a weight.

Let stand in room temperature, with the lid slightly off, for 1 day. Then store in the fridge with the lid on. Make sure the vegetables are covered by liquid the whole time.

ROOKIE STYLE FOR YOU

If you're short on time you can of course buy ready fermented vegetables. Make sure to buy unpasteurised as during pasteurisation much of the nutrients are lost.

4 portions as a side

CASHEW COLESLAW

50 g cashew nuts (soaked for four hours)
50 ml cold pressed olive oil
1 tbsp honey
1 tbsp light tahini
2 tbsp freshly squeezed lemon juice
1 garlic clove
100 ml water
4 carrots
½ red cabbage head
salt
freshly ground black pepper

An ordinary coleslaw contains crème fraiche and mayonnaise but since we like to challenge old traditions we make ours with cashew nuts and tahini. Yum!

Put the nuts into the food processor together with the olive oil, honey, tahini, lemon juice and one peeled crushed garlic clove. Add water and blend for about 1 minute till everything is wonderfully creamy. Season with salt and pepper.

Scrub the carrots. Grate them coarsely and finely shred the red cabbage. Stir the carrots, cabbage and cashew sauce together in a bowl.

1 small bowl

QUICK PICKLED RED ONION

1 red onion
100 ml water
2 tbsp apple cider vinegar
1 pinch salt

Onion, onion, onion. We and our Lukes love onion in every which way and one of the most delicious things we can think of is picked red onion.

Peel the onion and slice very thinly before placing in a bowl. Pour the water, vinegar and salt over the sliced onion. Let stand for 30 minutes. Squeeze the onion and pour off the extra liquid.

4 portions

INSTEAD OF ORDINARY MASH

Sweet potato and garlic puree
3 sweet potatoes (about 600 g)
1 small garlic clove
juice from 1 lemon
50-100 ml plant based milk of your choice
½ tsp salt
1 g freshly ground black pepper

Potato and Jerusalem artichoke mash
6 potatoes (about 500 g)
6 small Jerusalem artichokes (about 300 g)
1 g grated nutmeg
50-100 ml water (saved from boiling the root vegetables)
2 tsps nutritional yeast (optional)
½ tsp salt
1 g freshly ground white pepper

We've always loved mash. When we were little our mothers made it with butter and full fat milk but now that we're parents ourselves we're doing it a little differently. We've also discovered that mash is the perfect way to eat vegetables other than just potato.

Sweet potato and garlic puree
Boil the potatoes and garlic till they're soft enough to be mashed with a fork (takes about 30 minutes). Pour off the water and mix the sweet potato and garlic with the lemon juice. Then pour in the milk until the mash becomes a smooth puree. Season with salt and black pepper. Pour into a bowl and leave to cool in the fridge. Goes well with the beetroot burgers on page 95 amongst other things.

ROOKIE STYLE FOR YOU

This mash works just as well as a dip at a party as it does served alongside the main dish at dinner.

Potato and Jerusalem artichoke mash
Peel the root vegetables and cut into pieces. Boil in salted water till soft. Pour off most of the water (save a little to thin the mash with) and mash the root vegetables. Stir or whisk in the saved cooking water till the mash reaches the desired consistency.

Season with nutmeg, nutritional yeast, salt and white pepper. Works nicely with the fake fingers on page 92 and the fab patties on page 102.

ROOKIE STYLE FOR YOU

If your children think the mash is overwhelmed by the taste of the Jerusalem artichokes then start with half the amount. Or a fifth. Something is better than nothing!

4 portions

INSTEAD OF RICE

Buckwheat with tahini
200 g dried whole buckwheat
400 ml water
2 tsp tamari soya sauce
1 tsp cold pressed olive oil
2 tsp light tahini

Coconut quinoa
200 g white quinoa
200 ml coconut milk
200 ml water
2 g salt

Sorghum with lemon
200 g whole sorghum
400 ml water
1 lemon, peel from the whole
+ 2 tbsp juice
2 g salt

Many of our blog readers struggle to find nutritious alternatives for what we call tummy fillers (nutrient poor carbohydrates such as white rice and ordinary pasta). Here are our best tips for pimped up grains and corn that will raise the nutritional value of all your weekday meals.

Buckwheat with tahini
Boil the buckwheat in water and half of the tamari soya sauce. Let it boil till the liquid has been absorbed, this takes 10-15 minutes. Combine the rest of the soya sauce with the olive oil and tahini and stir into the buckwheat. Let cool. Keeps for 3 days in the fridge and works particularly well with the mango casserole on page 91.

Coconut quinoa
Boil the quinoa in the coconut milk and water. Boil till the liquid has been absorbed, this takes about 15 minutes. Keeps for 3 days in the fridge and works particularly well as an accompaniment to the bibimbap on page 122.

Sorghum with lemon
Soak the sorghum according to the instructions on the packet. Boil the sorghum with the lemon juice and salt in double the amount of water.

Boil till the water has been absorbed which will take about 35 minutes. Let cool and grate the lemon on top. Keeps in the fridge for 3 days and works well with all kinds of fish.

Prescription No. 4

FINE DINING

At the start of our pilgrimage we would differentiate between a special dinner and an everyday meal. We maintained our good habits from Monday to Friday and then at the weekends rewarded ourselves with everything we'd missed during the week.

But then we came to realise that the best way to spoil ourselves was with something that both tasted good and did good for our gut flora. Fine dining doesn't need to mean cream and fillet steak. And it really doesn't need to lead to stomach cramps and a food coma. Fine dining can just as well mean carefully sourced ingredients, lovingly prepared so as to maximise the pleasure for the body.

So, in this chapter we're killing two birds with one stone and offering both our guests and our good bacteria three festive three course menus.

4 starter portions

FOOD PHARMACY'S LUXURY SOUP

Carrot juice
1 small piece of ginger
1 lemongrass
200 ml freshly pressed carrot juice
3 tbsp rapeseed oil
3-4 tbsp freshly squeezed lime juice
salt

Salsa
½ small cucumber
6 plum tomatoes
½ avocado
1 red chilli
½ pot coriander
2 tbsp olive oil
salt
freshly ground black pepper

This might be one of the best starters we've ever eaten. In this book the soup is served vegan but as true Gothenburgers we often serve the soup with 200 g of fresh prawns. Some saltiness is never a bad thing!

Peel and chop the ginger, chop the lemongrass and put in a blender along with the carrot juice and rapeseed oil. Blend for about half a minute and season with lime and salt. Blend again before serving.

Dice the cucumber and tomatoes. Peel, remove the stone and dice the avocado. Deseed and finely chop the chilli. Mix with olive oil and roughly chopped coriander. Season with salt and pepper. Spoon the salsa into glasses or small bowls and then pour round the carrot juice.

ROOKIE STYLE FOR YOU

If you don't have a juicer at home you can of course make the dish with shop bought carrot juice.

100% RAW FOR YOU
ADD SHRIMP IF YOU LIKE
ADD FISH IF YOU LIKE

ADD SHRIMP IF YOU LIKE
ADD FISH IF YOU LIKE

4 portions

NOODLE SALAD WITH GREEN MANGO

Salad

1 green mango
2 carrots
2 spring onions (with stalks)
2 packets of kelp noodles (about 300 g)
250 g green soya beans
150 g natural peanuts
1 pot mint

Dressing

2 tbsp honey
juice from 2 squeezed limes
2 tbsp fish sauce
2 tbsp tamari soya sauce
4 tbsp sesame seed oil
1 tbsp water
4 cm fresh ginger without peel
1 garlic clove

To serve

Lime wedges

A common misunderstanding is that one should wait to eat fruit till it's ripe. We don't. When we go to the vegetable section we look for barely ripe mango and the greenest bananas. It's one of the reasons why our Lukes are in such a great mood these days.

Apologies to our friends having to eat this dish every time you come home to us but this is such a fantastically tasty noodle salad.

Start by peeling the mango and cutting it into matchsticks. Do the same with the carrots. Continue by slicing two spring onions finely. Rinse two packets of kelp noodles. Mix the noodles, mango, spring onion, carrot, soya beans, peanuts (save a few for decoration) and the mint (again, save a little for decoration).

Combine the honey, lime, fish sauce, soya sauce, sesame oil and water. Finely grate the ginger and chop the garlic and stir into the dressing. Taste.

Mix the noodle salad together with the dressing and slop everything onto a large plate. Drizzle over some extra soya sauce and sprinkle the mint and coarsely chopped peanuts on top. Serve with lime wedges.

QUICK TIP!

In the Physical realm lightly fry the peanuts in a frying pan for even more taste!

ROOKIE STYLE FOR YOU

Kelp noodles? Yup, they're made of seaweed and can be found in all good food supermarkets.

4-6 portions

GINO FOR THE GUT FLORA

"White chocolate"
35 g cacao butter
(50 ml melted)
1 tbsp cashew butter
1 tbsp honey
½ g vanilla powder
½ g salt

Fruit
2 green bananas
2 kiwi fruit
250 g strawberries
125 g blueberries
Mint for serving

On a backstreet in central Stockholm you'll find the classic neighbourhood restaurant PA&Co where we often finish off our dinners with the world's most delicious dessert: gino. So far so good, except for that your gut flora likes neither ice cream nor white chocolate.

So we experimented and created a healthy gino instead. This is for all the wonderful people out there who think that life's too short not to eat gino every day.

Melt the cacao butter in a bain-marie. Mix all the ingredients till smooth. Line a small, wide jar with baking paper and pour in the white chocolate sauce. Put in the fridge and leave to harden.

Preheat the oven to 100°C. Peel and slice the bananas and kiwi fruit, hull the strawberries and cut them in two. Put the fruit and berries into an oven-proof dish. Place the dish in the middle of the oven and bake for 30 minutes till everything is lightly warmed through.

Remove the fruit from the oven and grate over the "white chocolate", it will melt as it is served. Garnish with mint leaves.

ROOKIE STYLE FOR YOU

Cashew butter can be found in all good food shops. However if you can't get hold of it you can make your own: Soak 100g of cashew nuts for 4 hours. Pour off the water and blend to a smooth butter.

And!

If you want you can put the chocolate in the freezer instead of the fridge. It'll then take a little longer to melt.

ADD SHRIMP
IF YOU LIKE

4 starter portions (16 rolls)

SUMMER ROLLS

Rolls

200 g red cabbage
2 carrots
2 avocados
1 fresh mango
2 spring onions (with stalks)
½ green chilli
100 g sunflower sprouts
a few drops of freshly squeezed lime juice
1 pot of lemon balm
8 large rice papers (spring roll wrappers)

Dip

2 cm fresh ginger without peel
2 tbsp sesame oil
4 tbsp tamari soya sauce
grated peel and squeezed juice from 1 lime
1 tbsp white sesame seeds

Tamari mayonnaise

100 g mayonnaise (see page 53)
1 tbsp tamari soya sauce

This isn't just a fantastically tasty starter, nutritionally it also ticks many of our boxes: rainbow food, lots of raw vegetables, increased nutritional content in the form of sprouts and an anti-inflammatory dipping sauce.

Finely shred the red cabbage. Scrub the carrots and cut into matchsticks.

Cut the avocado in two and remove the stone. Scoop out and dice the flesh. Squeeze over a drop of lime juice so that the avocado doesn't brown. Peel and dice the mango. Finely slice the spring onions. Finely chop the chilli. Combine the avocado, mango, spring onions and chilli.

Wet a clean tea towel and squeeze the water out thoroughly. Fill a bowl or large pie dish with lukewarm water. Dip the rice paper wraps, one by one, into the water for about 30 seconds and and then place on the tea towel. Place the red cabbage, carrot sticks, sunflower sprouts, avocado and mango salsa in the middle of the wrap. Place a few lemon balm leaves on top. Fold the edges over the filling, tuck in the sides and roll up to a firm roll. Make the rest of the rolls in the same way. Cut the rolls in two and place them apart (so they don't stick together) on a dish.

Finely chop the ginger and mix with the rest of the ingredients to make the dipping sauce. Stir the tamari soya sauce into the mayonnaise. Pour into two bowls and place in the centre of the table.

4 portions

BIBIMBAP

1 packet firm natural tofu (about 270 g)
1 tbsp tamari soya sauce
1 tbsp sesame seed oil
1 tsp sambal oelek
4 portions coconut quinoa (see page 110)
50 g red cabbage
250 g green soya beans, defrosted
50 g mung bean sprouts
100 g kimchi (see page 106)
2 nori sheets
1 lime
fresh coriander

It only took us 39.5 years and two book contracts to understand that this dish isn't called bimbimbap. Thank you dear Editor Linnea for correcting this at the last minute, unfortunately when it comes to our mouths, they still aren't getting it...

Ordinary bumbumbop is made with rice, but we make our bopbopbam with fluffy coconut quinoa. There aren't really any rules, well actually yes, two – it should be eaten in a bowl and with a spoon!

Press the tofu by placing between two pieces of kitchen paper, under something heavy, for 20 minutes. Cut the tofu into slices.

Mix the tamari soya sauce, sesame oil and sambal oelek and pour over the tofu. Marinate for 20 minutes.

Heat the oven to 125°C. Place the slices on a baking tray covered in baking paper and bake in the oven for 20 minutes.

Divide the coconut quinoa between four deep bowls. Shred the red cabbage. Place the tofu, soya beans, red cabbage, mung bean sprouts and kimchi in small piles around the quinoa. Sprinkle over the coriander and the shredded nori sheets. Serve with a lime wedge and stir.

QUICK TIP!

The dip + mayo from the summer rolls on page 121 also work well with the bambambam!
And!
In the Physical realm we have been known to add some gochujang paste.

ADD SHRIMP IF YOU LIKE
ADD FISH IF YOU LIKE

100% RAW FOR YOU
UNDER 5 MINUTES

4 portions

PLATO'S MANGO PANNACOTTUS

Pannacotta
200 g fresh or thawed frozen mango
100 ml coconut milk
50 ml cold pressed coconut oil
1 tsp vanilla powder
1 tsp freshly squeezed lime juice

Topping
fresh mango
a few drops of lime juice
fresh mint

Plato looks at Mia and her son Ludde with elation.

– Attention, I have a delectabus recipe for a mango pannacottus.

Ludde lights up.

– Oh, could we have it?

– Of course. Take duo centum grams mango conti, an cocoes lacte centum millilitre...

– I don't understand a thing.

Mia interjects:

– Erm, thank you, but could you write it down instead?

– Of coursus!!

Mia runs up to the attic and digs out her old Latin textbook from 1995.

– Ha, I KNEW there'd be a use for this sooner or later!

Blend all the pannacotta ingredients and spoon into four small dessert bowls. Leave in the fridge for a few hours to set.

Peel and dice the mango. Take the pannacotta from the fridge and top with the mango, a few drops of lime juice and perhaps some mint. Please start!

4–6 starter portions

BEETROOT CARPACCIO WITH MUSTARD MAYONNAISE AND HAZELNUTS

500 g beetroots
100 g mayonnaise (see page 53)
2 tsp Dijon mustard
2 tsp honey
50 g hazelnuts
50 g rocket
1 tbsp freshly squeezed orange juice
½ tsp sea salt

Prepare this starter, taste and then fill in your rating here: ☆☆☆☆☆

Cut off the roots, leaves and stalks and scrub the beetroots. Use a mandolin or cheese slicer to make very thin slices. Place in ice cold water for ten minutes (for extra crispy slices). Pour off the water, dry the slices and lay out on a large, flat serving dish.

Make the mayonnaise and flavour with the mustard and honey.

Dollop the mayonnaise onto the beetroot slices. Roughly chop the hazelnuts and sprinkle over. Top with rocket and squeeze over the orange juice. Sprinkle with a good amount of sea salt.

ROOKIE STYLE FOR YOU

Test placing other vegetables in ice cold water for 10 minutes before serving for a nice, crisp exterior.

100% RAW FOR YOU

ADD SHRIMP
IF YOU LIKE

ADD FISH
IF YOU LIKE

4 portions

"BOUILLABAISSE"

Soup

1 yellow onion
½ leek
4 garlic cloves
5 tomatoes
a handful (about 100 g) mange tout peas
1 carrot
1 fennel
1.2 litres vegetable stock
juice from ½ orange
1 tbsp dried basil
1 tbsp dried thyme
1 bay leaf
1 packet (½ g) saffron
1 tin haricot beans (about 400 g)
2 tbsp finely chopped parsley
salt
freshly ground black pepper

Raw rouille

1 potato (raw)
2-3 garlic cloves
1 red pepper
1 tsp dried thyme
1 tsp dried basil
1 g cayenne pepper
50 ml olive oil
salt
freshly ground black pepper

We're about to do something we don't do very often, namely to boil all the vegetables. But to make amends we've added the raw anti-inflammatory superrouille to end all rouilles to enjoy with your soup. In most bouillabaisse recipes the vegetables are fried but there we draw the line. Restaurant owners of Marseilles should cover their ears now, we throw everything into a saucepan, boil it up and let it simmer for 10 minutes. Ready.

Peel and chop the onion, leek and garlic. Chop the tomatoes into large pieces. Cut the mange tout in half and slice the carrots and fennel.

Boil the stock together with the orange juice, dried herbs, saffron and vegetables. Once brought to the boil reduce to a gentle simmer until the vegetables have reached the right consistency (about 10 minutes). Season with salt and pepper.

Take the opportunity to make the rouille while you wait. Put everything into a food processor (the potato should be raw) and pulse till you reach the desired consistency.

Pour off the liquid from the haricot beans and rinse. Stir in the beans and chopped parsley just before serving with the rouille on the side.

ROOKIE STYLE FOR YOU

If you want to add prawns or fish, go for it! Throw them in at the end, a few minutes before serving. Or else put the prawns in a big bowl on the table and guests can do as they wish.

4 portions

CHOCOLATE MOUSSE EXTRAORDINAIRE

Mousse
10 dates (pitted)
100 g raw cacao powder
4 tbsp coconut cream
3 avocados

Topping
50 g buckwheat
fresh figs
fresh blueberries

If one likes metaphors one could say that cacao is nature's very own upper as it contains two substances known for their mood enhancing capabilities. And isn't that what we want at a dinner party?

Another of cacao's unique selling points is that it contains masses of flavonoids (a form of anti-oxidant) known for their high magnesium levels. Maybe not as fun at the dinner party but pretty good when the guests have gone home as magnesium helps you sleep well at night.

The absolute best thing about this dish though is of course the taste.

Heat the oven to 70°C. Place the buckwheat in a sieve. Boil water and pour it over the buckwheat. Let the water run off, spread the buckwheat out on a baking tray covered with baking paper and place in the oven. Stir every now and then. Remove when it looks ready and has become crispy, this takes about 2 hours.

Pulse the dates, cacao and coconut cream in a food processor. Add the avocado and continue till the mixture becomes soft and fluffy. Sample with an unnecessarily large spoon.

Dish up the chocolate mousse into four glasses and serve with blueberries, the crispy buckwheat and fresh figs cut into wedges.

ROOKIE STYLE FOR YOU

If you only have dried dates, you can leave them in water for a while so as to soften them.

Prescription No. 5

A COSY SATURDAY

Come on, you didn't really think you'd have to give up your weekend treats just because you're starting to feed your good bacteria? Forget it – we are going to get seriously cosy here. The only difference between our old Saturday night routine and our new is that we don't watch Strictly Come Dancing with Darth anymore, but with Luke.

One caveat though: When one makes something from this chapter it's easy to stuff oneself (it's all healthy, right?) We just want to point out that whilst these recipes are full of wholesome ingredients they still raise the blood sugar levels. So don't go wild. Don't eat the toffee balls for breakfast. But do for elevenses. End of lecture.

Please turn the page.

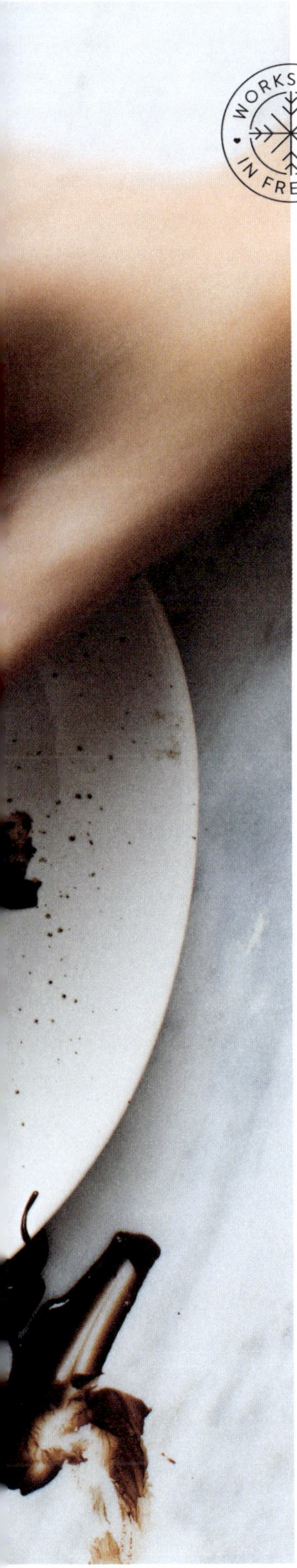

15 balls

FOOD PHARMACY'S TOFFEE BALLS

Those of you who follow our blog are guaranteed to have seen this recipe before. Maybe you're thinking: Oh come on, don't tell me they're dragging that old recipe out again?

It was never our plan to disappoint you. We just couldn't resist adding our favourite recipes to this book. Not to mention we're turning 40 soon which means we're becoming nostalgic. Most importantly though, this is one of the recipes which still leads to Hallelujah emails from blog readers, two years after we first posted it.

20 dates (pitted)
1 tsp salt
50 ml cold pressed coconut oil
1 tsp vanilla powder
dark chocolate (at least 70%)
small wooden kebab sticks

Put the dates into a blender together with the salt, coconut oil and vanilla powder. Pulse till everything becomes glossy and chewy. Roll the mixture into small balls.

Melt the chocolate in a bain-marie. Push a stick into each ball and then dip the balls quickly into the chocolate. Place the sticks in a glass until the chocolate has hardened completely. Remove the sticks from the balls.

Congratulations, you've reached the end. Pop one in your mouth immediately, they disappear fast.

QUICK TIP!

Dare to flavour the toffee with cardamom, liquorice powder or grated lemon peel.

About 15 squares

KARLEKSMUMS DELUXE

Base

200 g walnuts (soaked if possible)
200 g dates (pitted)
50 g raw cacao powder
1 tbsp nut butter of choice
1 pinch of salt
1 tsp water

Frosting

1 avocado
1 tsp vanilla powder
1 tbsp cold pressed coconut oil
2 tbsp raw cacao powder
3 tbsp honey
100 g desiccated coconut

These karleksmums (basically scrummy bites of love) have taken nearly 30 years to develop. Between 1987 and 1993 we experimented nearly every day after school with caster sugar, cocoa powder, egg and flour. Our goal then was to 1) calm our sugar cravings and 2) bake the world's most delicious chocolate cake. A few years ago we got going again but set the bar a little higher – we didn't just want to calm those sugar cravings with sticky cake, we wanted that same cake to contain antioxidants, fibre and good fats.

Mix the ingredients for the base. The dough should hang together and be a little sticky. Spread out somewhat evenly into a dish and place in the freezer.

Blend the avocado, vanilla, coconut oil, cacao powder and honey to a smooth frosting. Spread over the cake and leave to set in the fridge for about 1 hour.

Bring out, sprinkle over the coconut and cut into small squares.

ROOKIE STYLE FOR YOU

We always buy raw cacao as the beans have been heavily roasted in normal cocoa powder.

WORKS WELL
IN FREEZER

About 20 pieces (ie far too few)

LUKE SKYWALKER'S CINNAMON BUNS

Imagine a cinnamon bun. Peel off that dry outer layer. What have you got left? The middle. Imagine a cinnamon bun with only the middle. Are you with us? That is what we are going to bake today. And no, not in the oven.

"Bun dough"
200 g cashew nuts
100 g oats
100 g desiccated coconut
1 pinch salt
8 fresh dates (pitted)
3-4 tsp water

Filling
100 g sweet almonds (soaked if possible)
1 tbsp ground cinnamon
8 dates (pitted)
1 tbsp water

Roast the cashew nuts and oats in the oven for about 10 minutes at 100°C.

Make the bun dough in a blender and roll out between two pieces of baking paper.

Mix the filling and spread over the bun dough. Roll it up and chill quickly before cutting into large mouth sized pieces. Top with the desiccated coconut.

100% RAW FOR YOU
WORKS WELL IN FREEZER

Time for

THE STORY OF SOMEONE

Look! Someone has made us a green smoothie.

But, what's happened here? Someone has left crumbs on the kitchen surface. Who could it be?

We move on and find a trail of desiccated coconut on the stairs down to the cellar. Who could have done that?

Kitchen paper covered in sticky fingerprints! This just gets stranger and stranger...

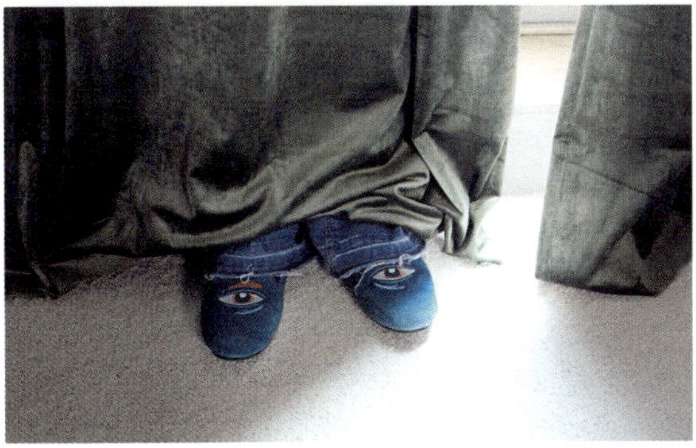

But look, someone is standing behind the curtains. What do you say, dare we look and see who it is?

GLOW

UNDER 5 MINUTES

WORKS WELL IN FREEZER

About 10 balls

THE WORLD'S BEST CHOCOLATE BALLS

After hundreds of tasting sessions we hereby announce that we have decided on the best recipe for chocolate balls, in all categories. So delicious you won't want to share.

7 dates (pitted)
200 g oats
3 tbsp cold pressed coconut oil
2 tbsp raw cacao powder
50 g desiccated coconut and 100g for rolling in
1 pinch of salt
1 dash of cold coffee

Combine everything in a food processor. Shape the batter into small balls and roll in the coconut.

100% RAW FOR YOU
WORKS WELL IN FREEZER

A little jar

ROCKY ROAD

100 g natural peanuts
100 g dried goji berries
100 g desiccated coconut
1-2 pinches of salt
10 dates (pitted)
2 tbsp + 100 ml cold pressed coconut oil
100 g raw cacao powder
50 ml honey

Congratulations! Here, for your delectation, is our friend Charlotte's recipe for the world's tastiest sweet. God, we get goosebumps just thinking about it. It's made in 3 ½ steps but don't let that scare you off.

Step 1 – Nut mix
This is the simplest (and least sticky) part. Mix together the peanuts, goji berries, coconut and a pinch of salt.

Step 2 – Toffee
Put the dates, 2 tablespoons of coconut oil and the tiniest pinch of salt in a food processor and pulse till it becomes a chewy toffee. It takes longer than you'd probably imagine it would – just when you think you're done, pulse a little more. When you have a chewy toffee right under your nose put it into the fridge (the toffee, not the nose).

Step 3 – Chocolate
Melt 100 grams of coconut oil in a bain-marie together with the cacao and honey and taste. If you want it even sweeter you can add a little more honey, but remember you'll be mixing in the toffee soon which will also add sweetness.

Step 3 ½ - Throw everything together
Speaking of the toffee – take it out of the fridge and break into smaller pieces. Stir the toffee pieces and nut mix into the chocolate and spread the mixture onto a piece of baking paper. Place it in the fridge and leave to harden for a few hours. Take out the chocolate and break into good sized pieces.

SCIENCE FOR YOU

Goji berries are heavily sprayed so make sure you use organic. If you can't get hold of that use dried mulberries instead.

16 squares

LUKE SKYWALKER'S GRANOLA SQUARES

Granola

200 g whole buckwheat
100 g chopped sweet almonds
100 g chopped walnuts
100 g pumpkin seeds
50 g linseeds
50 g white sesame seeds
50 g desiccated coconut
2 tsp ground cinnamon
2 tsp ground cardamom
3 tbsp soft cold pressed coconut oil

Mixture

8 dates (pitted)
3 tbsp cold pressed coconut oil

In our last book we shared our favourite granola recipe. And it's not just us, our children, Emil, Rajraj, friends, neighbours, singing coaches, masseurs and ballet teachers who love them – Luke and his army cheer as soon as we approach the granola jar.

This recipe is a variation where we just add a few dates and in a jiffy you have a pile of amazingly tasty granola squares for tea. Even yummier than sweets!

Soak the buckwheat for 30 minutes.

Heat the oven to 70°C. Chop the almonds and walnuts. Mix all the ingredients together and spread out over a piece of baking paper on a baking tray and place in the oven. Wait a couple of hours, stir every now and again and remove when the granola feels dry and the whole kitchen smells of cinnamon. Leave to cool.

Mix 50 grams of the granola with the dates and the coconut oil in a food processor till combined. Press down into a small cake tin and place into the fridge for 1 hour to harden.

Remove and cut into bite size pieces. Store in the fridge in a jar with a tightly fitting lid.

ROOKIE STYLE FOR YOU

If you don't have the time or energy to make your own granola it's fine to buy ready made. Just make sure it doesn't have added sugar!

QUICK TIP!

If you want to make the squares less sweet you can use fewer dates.

WORKS WELL IN FREEZER

2–4 portions

THREE KINDS OF FRUIT SALAD

Fruit salad
1 green banana
1 orange
2 kiwi fruit
2 fresh figs
1 pear

Vanilla sauce (about 300 ml)
150 g cashew nuts (soaked for at least 4 hours)
150 ml water
2 dates (pitted)
½ tsp vanilla powder

Caramel sauce (about 300 ml)
10 dates (pitted)
200 ml plant based milk of choice
2 pinches salt
1 g vanilla powder

Chocolate sauce (about 300 ml)
100 ml melted cold pressed coconut oil.
100 g raw cacao powder
50 ml honey
l g sea salt

Now we might not be professional mind readers but something tells us that you're thinking about hopping over this recipe because fruit salad sounds a little boring. Don't do it. Because it's not the fruit that is the star of this recipe, it's the sauces.

Or as Mia's daughter Juni usually says,

"Mummy, I don't need any fruit with my fruit salad today."

Make the sauces in a blender.

Slice the fruit and top with one or more of the sauces.

SCIENCE FOR YOU

Remember to use at least three colours of fruit (at least if you want the maximum health benefits).

And!

Many people worry that they are eating too much fruit but to be honest it's not high fruit consumption that's the problem with our diet today – in fact it's the opposite, most of us would do well from eating more fruit. However if you're still concerned about eating too much think about that the more sour the fruit (grapefruit for example), the lower the sugar content.

Time for

TEAM BUILDING

We feel now is the time for us to do a group exercise with you to bind us together. Make us more of a team.

1.
Trust us and bring out 2 dates, 1 tbsp coconut oil, 1 tsp vanilla powder, 2 tbsp raw cacao powder and 400 ml plant milk.

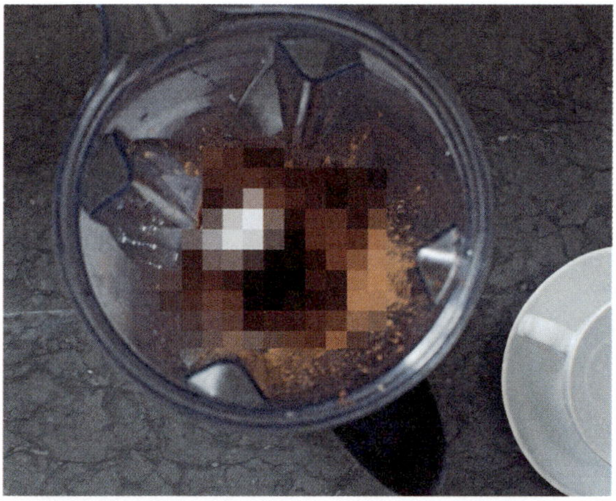

2.
Trust us and put these ingredients in a blender.

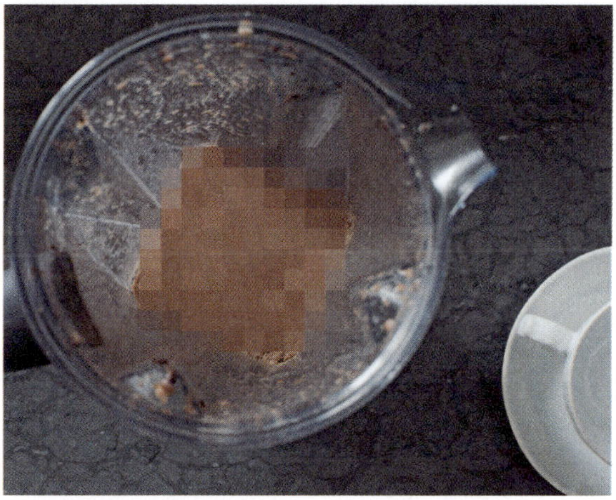

3.
Press start. And yes, you can still trust us.

4.
Pour the contents of the blender into a saucepan and heat carefully. Doesn't it feel like we've come a little closer now?

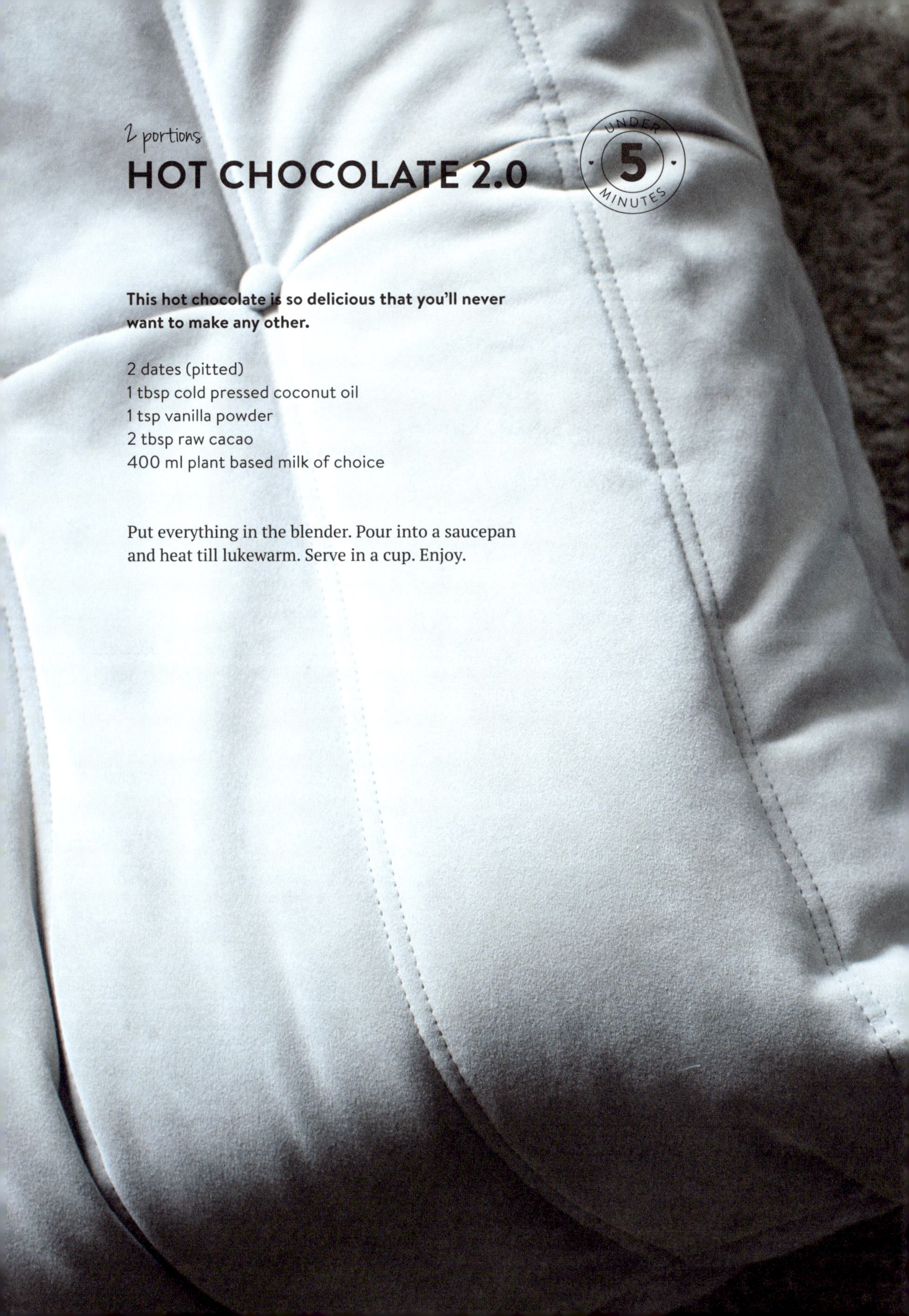

2 portions

HOT CHOCOLATE 2.0

UNDER 5 MINUTES

This hot chocolate is so delicious that you'll never want to make any other.

2 dates (pitted)
1 tbsp cold pressed coconut oil
1 tsp vanilla powder
2 tbsp raw cacao
400 ml plant based milk of choice

Put everything in the blender. Pour into a saucepan and heat till lukewarm. Serve in a cup. Enjoy.

E 180 EQ
BASF
E 180
SPLASH
E.T.
E 180
QUALITY GRADE
PHILIPS
Made in Austria – Fabriqué en Autriche
CROCODILE DUNDEE II
DIRTY DANCING
PRO & VI DOC
KONFIRMATION
Gustavi Domkyrka 8 augusti 1992
PRO & VI DOC
THE BLUE LAGOON
GREMLINS
E 180
Pretty Woman

SEED CRISPS WITH DIPS

Seed crisps (2 trays)
200 g almond flour
100 g white sesame seeds
100 g sunflower seeds
100 g pumpkin seeds
50 g linseeds
3 tbsp psyllium husk
½ tsp fine salt + sea salt to sprinkle over
200 ml water
50 ml cold pressed coconut oil

Kiwi jam (1 small bowl)
4 kiwi fruit
3 dates (pitted)
1 tbsp freshly squeezed lime juice
1 g vanilla powder
3 tbsp chia seeds

Red pesto dip (1 small bowl)
40 g sundried tomatoes
12 plum tomatoes
100 g walnuts (soaked if possible)
50 ml cold pressed olive oil
1 tbsp freshly squeezed lemon juice
1 pot basil
salt
freshly ground black pepper

ROOKIE STYLE FOR YOU

When heating oil we nearly always use coconut, but in the Physical realm we do make kale crisps (page 40) and seed crisps with olive oil.

Lina loves crisps. And since Lina loves crisps there's never been a question of her giving them up, we just had to find another way. So we discovered seed crisps. And now Lina loves them instead.

Great together with our kiwi jam, pesto dip and Mr Gere.

Seed crisps

Combine all the dry ingredients.

Boil the water and pour over the dry mixture together with the oil. Mix well. Divide between two pieces of baking paper, and place more baking paper on top. Roll out to a thin layer. Remove the top sheets of baking paper, sprinkle over the sea salt and press down gently so that the salt sticks. Replace the sheets of baking paper and let the trays stand for at least 2 hours, but preferably overnight.

Heat the oven to 80°C. Bake the seed mixture in the middle of the oven for 1 hour, remove the baking tray and turn the whole seed bake over and place directly onto the metal rack in the oven. Bake for another hour till completely dry and crispy. Do the same with the second baking tray. Keeps for up to 2 weeks in an airtight container.

Kiwi jam

Peel the kiwi fruit and cut into pieces. Blend the dates, lime juice, vanilla and half of the kiwi fruit to an almost smooth paste.

Add the rest of the kiwi fruit and pulse a few times, so that you get a chunkier mix. Stir in the chia seeds and place in the fridge. Leave to swell for at least 2 hours, till you have a jam like consistency.

Red pesto dip

Run all the ingredients through the blender.

A quite large bowl, about 500 g

FOOD PHARMACY'S BRIDGE MIX*

Herb roasted chickpea mix
1 tin chickpeas (400 g)
1 tbsp cold pressed coconut oil
½ tsp salt
½ tsp dried thyme
½ tsp dried basil

Semi-spicy tamari nuts
200 g mixed natural nuts (soaked if possible)
2 tbsp tamari soya sauce
1 tsp honey
1-2 g cayenne pepper

Dried berries
100 g dried mulberries

Go ahead and dig into the world's scrummiest bridge mix which, just like a classic bridge mix, contains a combination of tastes, shapes and consistencies. In the Realm of Ideas we don't eat honey, but a little teaspoon here or there has never hurt. Especially not on our tamari roasted nuts. The opposite in fact, there it has added spoonfuls of sunshine.

Heat the oven to 80°C. Pour off and rinse the chickpeas. Place on a baking tray and dry with a clean tea towel. Drizzle over the coconut oil and salt. Stir. Roast in the middle of the oven for 2 hours, shaking the tray now and again, till the chickpeas have turned lightly golden and have a crispy exterior. Leave to cool.

When an hour has passed, dry the nuts thoroughly with a tea towel (if soaked). Place in a bowl and pour over the honey and tamari soya sauce. Leave to marinate for 15 minutes.

Pour off the marinade and add the nut mix to the baking tray alongside the chickpeas. Roast in the middle of the oven for about 45 minutes, till the nuts are completely dry. Shake the tray now and again.

Pour the nut mix and cayenne pepper into a bowl and stir well. Mix in the chickpeas and add the dried herbs and mulberries.

*** "Bridge mix" is a Swedish classic, a mix of sugar or chocolate coated liquorice, mints, nuts, raisins, chocolate discs and puffed rice.**

SCIENCE FOR YOU

We love cashew nuts. They contain important minerals and vitamins, such as magnesium which helps our nerves and muscles to function as they should.

RECIPES

CATEGORY INDEX

THANK YOU

FOODPHARMACYCO.COM
WELCOME!

A big thank you to our beloved families and dear friends…
If we don't name anyone, then we won't forget anyone (not even you Chant).

A special thank you to Cervera, Ninni and all the wonderful blog readers out there. Without you, there would be no blog. Or cookbook.